Two *Treasurers* of the Late Middle Kingdom

Wolfram Grajetzki

BAR International Series 1007
2001

Published in 2016 by
BAR Publishing, Oxford

BAR International Series 1007

Two Treasurers *of the Late Middle Kingdom*

ISBN 978 1 84171 286 4

BAR Publishing is the trading name of British Archaeological Reports (Oxford) Ltd. British Archaeological Reports was first incorporated in 1974 to publish the BAR Series, International and British. In 1992 Hadrian Books Ltd became part of the BAR group. This volume was originally published by Archaeopress in conjunction with British Archaeological Reports (Oxford) Ltd / Hadrian Books Ltd, the Series principal publisher, in 2001. This present volume is published by BAR Publishing, 2016.

Printed in England

BAR
PUBLISHING

BAR titles are available from:

BAR Publishing
122 Banbury Rd, Oxford, OX2 7BP, UK
EMAIL info@barpublishing.com
PHONE +44 (0)1865 310431
FAX +44 (0)1865 316916
www.barpublishing.com

In my book on the high officials of the Middle Kingdom (W. Grajetzki, Die höchsten Beamten der ägyptischen Zentralverwaltung. Berlin 2000) I collected published sources and only very few unpublished monuments. There are still numerous unpublished stelae, statues, scarabs and other objects in museums, which are important for the prosopography of the high officials of the Middle Kingdom. These sources could complete our picture of that time. In the present volume I want to publish some of these sources. Another reason for writing this book is to reverse the proposed sequence of the treasurers *Snb-sw-m-ʿ(.j)* and *Snbj* from that published in my previous study, a point drawn to my attention by Detlef Franke. I am grateful to Franke for discussion of this matter. In the following book they will hopefully find a better place in history, even though there is still much research to do, to determine their exact place. This is not a classical study on administration. Although titles and their functions will be discussed, the focus of this work will be the relation of different social levels in the mid 13th Dynasty to each other.

I would like to thank the Institute of Egyptology in Mainz and Stephen Quirke for encouraging me in my work in several ways. I am grateful to the latter and especially to Jake Wilson for reading my English. All errors remain of course my responsibility. For further help I am also grateful to Sally-Ann Ashton and Nicholas Reeves.

For sending me pictures and similar help I am grateful to: Dr. Andrey O. Bolshakov (St. Petersburg), Julia McLaughlin Cook (Liverpool), John Deaton (Virginia Museum of Fine Arts in Richmond), Gisèle Pierini (Marseille), Dr. Angelika Lohwasser, Dr. I. Müller and Prof. Dr. Dietrich Wildung (Berlin), Dr. Jaromir Malek (Oxford), Dr. Helmut Satzinger (Vienna), Susanne Woodhouse (London).

Contents

Introduction

I.
The Middle Kingdom is in many respects the classical period of ancient Egyptian history and culture. This is not only true for the language and literature, but also for arts and even for political history. The Middle Kingdom can be divided into two main periods. The Early Middle Kingdom includes the 11th Dynasty from the unification of the country under Mentuhotep II and the 12th Dynasty until the reign of Senusret II. The Late Middle Kingdom starts with Senusret III, who seems to have reorganised the administration of the whole country. Many new titles appear on monuments of his time. There seems to be an increase in stelae production and scarab seals with name and titles come into use. However, there are not only changes in the administration. The entire material culture of the country changes. The model figures in the tombs and the coffin texts disappear, and other items such as shabtis or magical wands take their place.

Compared with other periods of Egyptian history the 12th Dynasty seems to be a period of great political stability with its many kings and long reigns. In stark contrast to the 12th Dynasty is the 13th Dynasty, a period with a long chain of short-reigning kings. Although considerable energy has been put by many researchers into arranging these kings, numerous problems still remain concerning the order of their succession. Most of the kings are not very well-attested and almost nothing is known about their background, their families and the reasons why they might have become king. At present, there is not even any general agreement on the question of who was the first king of the Dynasty. The Turin Kinglist places Khutauire at the start of the Dynasty (Ryholt 1997: 71, fig. 10), but Ryholt (1997: 315-320) has argued from his assessment of the sources that the copyist confused king Khutauire and Sekhemre-khutaui and that the latter should be identified as the first king if the 13th Dynasty. The same problems arise with the rulers immediately following the first king, so that there is no consensus in the scholarly literature on the order of succession of these rulers. The picture changes in about the middle of the 13th Dynasty. At that time there is suddenly a group of well-attested kings. Many monuments survive from both them and their officials, and even the family relations of some of these kings are quite clear. At least two of these kings reigned for about ten years.

This group consists of the following kings (nomen, prenomen, highest year date, attested in a contemporary source, and, in brackets, reign length given in the Turin Kinglist papyrus):

Sobekhotep II (Amenemhat) Sekhemre-khutaui	year 3
Khendjer Userkare	year 5
Mermesha Semenkhkare	
Antef (V) Sehetepkare	
Seth Meribre	
Sobekhotep III Sekhemre-sewadjtaui	year 1 (3)
Neferhotep I Khasekhemre	year 2 (11)
Sobekhotep IV Khaneferre	year 9
Sobekhotep V Khahotepre	(4)

It is not securely known how long these kings ruled. However, it is not impossible that Mermesha, Antef (V) and Seth might have reigned in total less than one year. From Antef (V) and Mermesha respectively only one and two statues survived and for king Seth there are no contemporary sources at all. In this light it should be pointed out that the whole period represented by these ten reigns might cover only about 35 years. Most of the datable monuments of the 13th Dynasty were set up by officials belonging to this period. Almost nothing is known about the rulers before this group of kings and the length of their reigns, but these earlier kings might have reigned about the same length of time (compare von Beckerath 1964: 222, 1785-1744 BC (41 years) from beginning of 13th Dynasty to Sobekhotep III; Ryholt 1997: 408, 1803 - 1764 BC (39 years) from beginning of the 13th Dynasty to Khendjer). Just as very little is known about these earlier 13th Dynasty kings, so it is extremely hard to say anything about the administration or the officials in this period.

As regards the kingship in the 13th Dynasty, the general opinion has always been that it was very unstable. The administration on the other hand is considered to have been relatively stable. The prototype for this stability was the office of the *vizier*. In particular the famous *vizier ʿnḫw*, who was the son of a *vizier* and the father of two other *viziers*, is treated almost as a kingmaker, who stayed in office longer than many kings whom he served (von Beckerath 1964: 99-100). Quirke (1991) pointed out that the powerful *viziers* are only known from the times of more powerful kings, i.e. precisely the period of the above-mentioned kings. From examination of the surviving sources and monuments it becomes clear that there are also other offices that might have been just as influential as the *vizier*. In particular the position of the *treasurer (jmj-rꜣ ḫtmt)* seems to have been very important in the 13th Dynasty.

The office of the *treasurer* was established in the Early Middle Kingdom as one of the highest offices at the royal palace (Helck 1958: 77-88). Several sources demonstrate the influential position of these people, notably the huge and costly tombs of some *treasurers*, the high number of their surviving monuments, some biographical inscriptions and other important titles. In my study of the high officials in the Middle Kingdom (Grajetzki 2000: 43-78) I hoped to show that the *treasurer* was after the *vizier* the most important official in the administration of the Middle Kingdom. It was possible to establish that the administration of the royal palace was divided into an economic part, of which the *treasurer* was the head, and an administrative/organisational part of which the *vizier* was the head. The *treasurer* played a more important part in the administration of the country in the Middle Kingdom than in any other period. Only in the early 18th Dynasty did the *treasurers* still belong to the highest courtiers, though they seem not to have been members of the very highest group (Engelmann-von Carnap 1999: 78, Abb. 53A shows the tomb size of the important officials in the mid 18th Dynasty- the *treasurer* figures in the group of officials with the second largest tomb size). In the time after Amenhotep III the office became relatively unimportant and seems to be replaced in function by the *overseer of the treasury*. A list of people from the Middle Kingdom with the title *treasurer* sounds almost like a roll-call of the most famous men of the time. In the tomb of *Mkt-Rꜥw* the superb wooden models were found, that are now in Cairo and New York. *Mnṯw-ḥtp* is famous for his series of statues from Karnak and his recently discovered tomb at Lisht. *Jjj-ḫr-nfrt* is known from his stela in Berlin, where he reports the arrangement of key rituals relating to Osiris. From *Ḥꜣr* there are more seals known than from any other individual of the Middle Kingdom. Finally, there are the *treasurers Snb-sw-m-ꜥ(.j)* and *Snbj*. They are both datable between the reigns of the kings Sobekhotep II and Sobekhotep IV. For *Snb-sw-m-ꜥ(.j)* there are more stelae known than for any other person from the Middle Kingdom. He is also known from a fine bronze statue and is mentioned on a group of Lahun papyri fragments. Both *treasurers* must have played an important role in their time. The need for a study on these two *treasurers* has already been pointed out several times (compare already Berlev 1978: 276; de Meulenaere 1981; Franke 1984: 8). New sources published in the meantime have made this even more important.

II.

It is not only the number of monuments of the *treasurers Snb-sw-m-ꜥ(.j)* and *Snbj* that is remarkable. The number of people mentioned on their stelae is also unusually high. It is clear that many of these officials worked together with or under the *treasurers*. They are also known from other monuments: first and foremost from stelae, but also from seals and statues. Through their connections with the two *treasurers* it is possible to create a dense network of social relationships for the mid 13th Dynasty. Indeed, the well established prosopography of the period from king Sobekhotep III to Sobekhotep IV (Franke 1984: 8, 15) depends principally precisely on the stelae relating to these two *treasurers*.

III.

In accordance with the high status of the *treasurer* in the Middle Kingdom it is not surprising to see that the *treasurers* are in most cases the main persons on their stelae. Most of them are placed in a prominent position on them, sitting on a chair on the left side in the upper register. People sitting on the left side (or not so often sitting alone on the right side) will be called "main person" or "person in the main position" in the present study. Quite often a second person is shown in front of the *treasurer*, *making a king's offering (jrt ḥtp-dj-njswt)*. This person seems to be the second most important on a stela and was presumably just under the *treasurer* in rank. They occupy the place of the eldest son who appears on many stelae of the Early Middle Kingdom and also very often still on stelae of the 13th Dynasty (for example: Berlin 1192, Berlin 7731, Cairo CG 20515, CG 20542, CG 20567, CG 20751, Florence 2504). These people will be called "person in the second position" or "offering man". They are often called *his child - ẖrd.f*. From different sources it is certain that they are not really the sons of the stelae owners. In his discussion of the attestations, Franke comes to the conclusion, following Berlev, that these are persons who grew up in the houses of their masters and for that reason were called *his child*, since their master would have been some kind of father to them (*ẖrd.f* see Franke 1983a: 304-308). For all other people mentioned on the stelae it is often quite difficult to say precisely what position they occupy in relation to the owner of the stela. In general, one gains the impression that they are in some way lower in position and rank, but there are examples where a higher person or a person equal in rank to the main person is mentioned in such a position (Munich GL WAF 34).

On some stelae two persons are shown sitting facing each other (for example: Tübingen 479, Leiden 30, London BM 903, Vienna ÄS 180). Such stelae give the impression that the two people are of equal rank and position. In these cases it is hard to say who was the more important of the two. One may even suppose that they really are equal in their social position, although there are some stelae where this is obviously not the case (for example Cairo CG 20570 where a *vizier* is sitting in front of an *jmj-rꜣ šnṯ*). Normally it can be assumed that the person sitting on the left is more important (compare for example the stelae where the man is sitting on the left and his wife on the right - Pittsburgh Acc. 21538-38; St. Petersburg Hermitage 1088; see also St. Petersburg Hermitage 1081, where the owner of the stela is sitting on the left; his father is sitting on the right; a similar case: Florence 2506). Another indicator for the more important person is who is mentioned first in the offering formula. Many stelae where two people are sitting in front of each other name only one of the two in the offering formula. It seems clear that the person mentioned in the offering formula is the main beneficiary of the stela (for example: Cairo CG 20075, Vienna ÄS 204). Some stelae include two offering formulae, arranged side by side in the roundel.

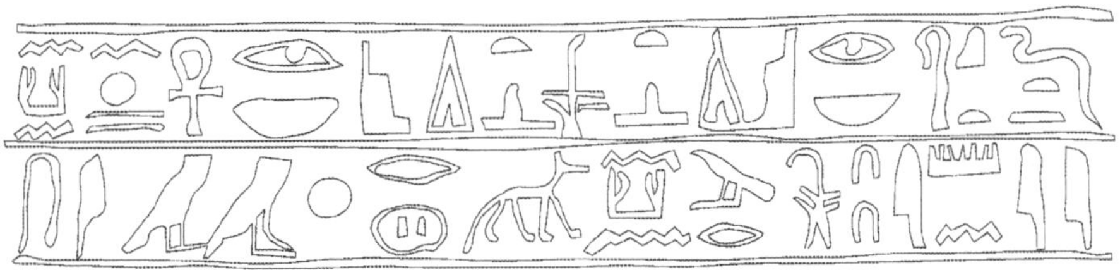

stela Vienna ÄS 102: two different offering formulae addressing two different people

Here one gets the strong impression that both people are equal in rank, even if one of them is sitting on the left side of the stela, which is inevitably the case (Cairo CG 20570, Florence 2523, Leiden 50, Tübingen 463, Vienna ÄS 133, ÄS 160, ÄS 172). It is therefore in general assumed that both are colleagues who are more or less equal in rank and who might have both jointly commissioned the production of the stela.

IV.

The stelae connected with *Snb-sw-m-ᶜ(.j)* and *Snbj* can be arranged for study in several groups according to the relationship of the officials mentioned on the stelae to the *treasurers*:

1. Stelae on which the *treasurers* themselves are mentioned. The stelae of this group will be the starting point for the following research. On many of these stelae, especially those of *Snb-sw-m-ᶜ(.j)* a person is shown offering in front of the *treasurer*. This is the person here called "person/official in the second position". The stelae of *Snbj* are slightly different. Here, the person in the second position is shown sitting in front of the *treasurer* (Plate 3).

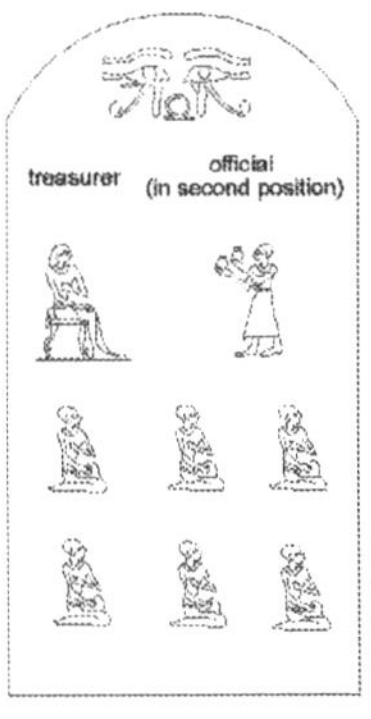

2. Stelae on which people who occupy the second position from group one are shown sitting in the first position.

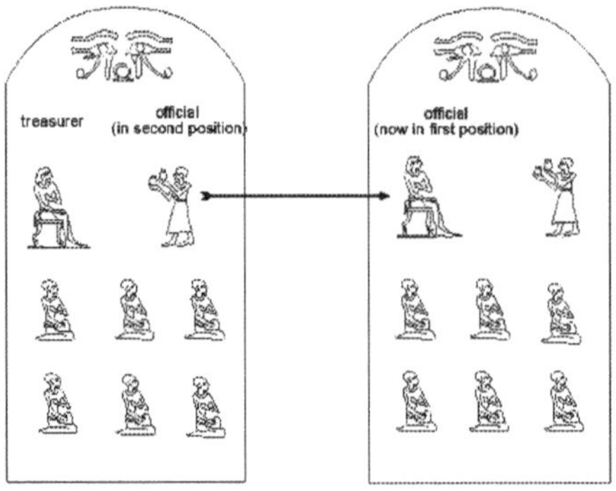

3. Stelae with people already known from group one who do not occupy the first or second position of the stelae in group one. On stelae of group 3 they can appear in any position.

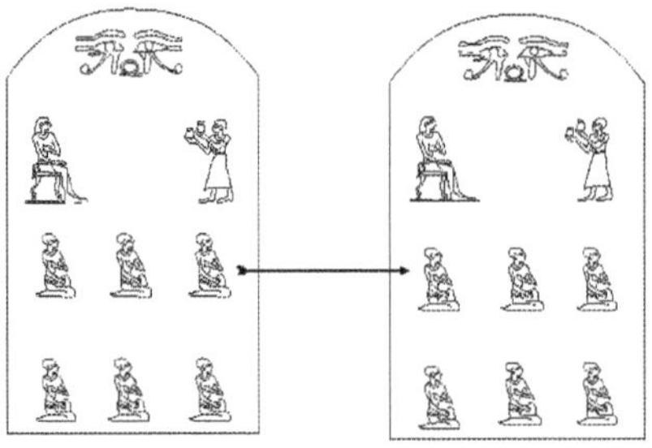

4. Stelae and monuments from/with people, who are mentioned on stelae of group 2 or 3, but not in the second position. The people of this group will not be considered further in this study, though a list of other monuments and stelae connected with the above-mentioned groups will be given.

The following chapters focus on the stelae in the first three groups. Although other material is included in this study, such as seals, statues, rock inscriptions and papyrus documents, the stelae form the core source material.

Chapter 1
Identities

This book is concerned mainly with the *treasurers Snb-sw-m-ʿ(.j)* and *Snbj* and the people attested around them. The first question which will arise for somebody who knows nothing about these high officials is that of the identity of people with identical names attested on different objects. Do all monuments with the name *Snb-sw-m-ʿ(.j)* and the title *jmj-rꜣ ẖtmt* belong to the same person, or are there a number of different people with this name and this title? Franke (1984: 5-6) has already discussed the possibility of identity and non-identity of people with the same name in the Middle Kingdom. In general, a single rule can be made, that the more identical or almost identical information on a person is available, the higher the chance that we are dealing with one individual. However, the less information available, the higher the chance that we are dealing with different people. It should also be taken into account that it is harder to distinguish people with popular names. Two extreme examples may illustrate this problem. There is a *treasurer* with the very common name *Snb*. He is shown on his stela (Vienna ÄS 145) - his only surviving monument as *treasurer* - sitting in front of a man and a woman. The man in front of him is called *Snb.tjfj*(not *Snb* as Grajetzki 2000: 59). The woman is called *Rn-snb*. There is also a *zẖꜣw n pr-ḥḏ* called *Snb*, known from different monuments (Franke, Doss. 611). His mother is also called *Rn-snb*. However as both names (*Rn-snb*, *Snb*) are very popular in the 13th Dynasty, the identity is highly speculative. On the other hand there is the case of an *jmj-rꜣ ẖnrt Sbk-ʿꜣ Bbj*, who is very likely identical with the similarly named *vizier* (Martin 1971: nos.1385, 1383-84; Vernus 1986: 57, no. 263). The identification seems to be secure even though the person is recorded with different titles: the name *Sbk-ʿꜣ* is quite common, but the double name *Sbk-ʿꜣ Bbj* seems not to be attested outside these two examples (Vernus 1986: 57, no. 263).

The cases of the two *treasurers* who will be discussed here are more complicated. *Snb-sw-m-ʿ(.j)* seems to be a popular name in the 13th Dynasty, but not so common as names such as Sobekhotep or Ameny. In all instances where a filiation for the *treasurer Snb-sw-m-ʿ(.j)* is given, his mother is always named as *Srwẖ-jb*. The name of his father is never recorded. There is no real reason to think that there might be more than two *treasurers* with the same name, in particular as there are numerous people on different stelae who are always connected with him. The only doubt may be the existence of some seals of *Snb-sw-m-ʿ(.j)* (Martin 1971: nos. 1513-1514; Quirke/Fitton 1997: 427, 437, n. 67) which are so different in type from his other seals that one has the impression that they do not belong to the same person. However, the seals may simply come from a different workshop or from the very beginning or very end of his career. There is also a *high steward* with the name *Snb-sw-m-ʿ(.j)*, whose mother is also called *Srwẖ-jb*. The name of his father is *Wpw-wꜣjwt-ḥtp*. From these names it seems to be highly likely that the *high steward* and the *treasurer* are identical. However, the case becomes much more complicated when examining other sources mentioning people with the name *Snb-sw-m-ʿ(.j)*. On a stela in Paris (Bibliotheque Nationale, cat. no.16) there is a person with that name and the title *zẖꜣw n ẖnrt wr*, whose mother is also called *Srwẖ-jb* but whose father is called *Jjj-ʿnẖ* (Franke, Doss. 666). Finally there is a *wr mḏw Šmʿw Snb-sw-m-ʿ(.j)* with a mother *Srwẖ-jb* on a stela from Esna, but whose father is called *Zꜣ-Mnṯw* (Franke 1983a: 23, n.1). As long as the name of the father of the *treasurer Snb-sw-m-ʿ(.j)* is unknown, it must remain an open question who is really to be identified with whom. It must also be taken into consideration that the father could possibly have had a double or even a triple name. If this is true all attestations of a person with the name *Snb-sw-m-ʿ(.j)* and a mother called *Srwẖ-jb* could refer to the same man. As already mentioned, the name *Snb-sw-m-ʿ(.j)* is quite popular in the 13th Dynasty, and even around the *treasurer Snb-sw-m-ʿ(.j)* himself we find other people named *Snb-sw-m-ʿ(.j)* who bear minor titles.

In the following list all examples of the name *Snb-sw-m-ʿ(.j)* have been collected from the available sources.

1. the *treasurer*
2. the *high steward*
3. *ẖrd n kꜣp* — stela Vienna ÄS 142; seal Martin 1971: no. 1511 (Franke, Doss. 663). The stela in Vienna might date under the *treasurer Snb-sw-m-ʿ(.j)* (the *zẖꜣw n ḫntj Jjj* appears here and on stela Cairo CG 20023)
4. *qnbtj n w* — stela Cairo CG 20540 (without title); stela Odessa GAM. inv. no. 52970 (Andreu 1991: 22; Franke, Doss. 662. Father: *Bw-rẖ.f*, mother: *Ṯn.tw-jb*)

5. *ḥkꜣjj n kꜣp*	stela Copenhagen National Museum Aad 10; New York, Brooklyn Museum. acc. no. 08.480.176 (Franke, Doss. 664)
6. *wr mḏw Šmꜥw* (father: *Zꜣ-Mnṯw*, mother: *Srwḫ-jb*)	stela Esna (Downes 1974: 80-81, no. 267E; Franke 1983a: 23, n.1)
7. *zꜣb*	stela Cairo CG 20724 (mother: *Ḥnwt-pw;* Franke, Doss. 665)
8. *zꜣb*	stela Cairo CG 20154 (Franke, Doss. 665)
9. *zẖꜣw n ẖnrt wr*	stela Paris, Bibliothèque Nationale, Cat. no. 16 (Franke, Doss. 666a)
10. *wdpw*	stela Roanne 163; Zagreb no. 8 (servant of the *treasurer Snb-sw-m-ꜥ(.j)*)
11. *zꜣw-ḥnkt*	stela London BM 238 (servant of the *treasurer* ?)
12. without title,	stela Pittsburgh Acc.2983-6701 (servant of the *treasurer*)
10-12 might refer to the same person	
13. *šmsw*	stela Rio de Janeiro 633 [2425] (Kitchen 1990: no. 9)
14. *jmj-rꜣ st*	stela Cairo CG 20562
15. *wšꜥ ꜣpdw* (a title ?)	stela Cairo CG 20656
16. title ?	stela Berlin 7286 (datable under *Snbj*; therefore after the *treasurer Snb-sw-m-ꜥ(.j)*)
17. *jdnw n sḏmw rmṯ*	seal Moscow GM. no. 6758 (mentioned by Franke 1982: 52)
18. *without title,*	stela London Petrie Museum UC 14456, (Stewart 1979: 32, no. 136, pl. 34.1)

The name *Snb-sw-m-ꜥ(.j)* seems not to be attested in the 12th Dynasty or earlier. Although the exact dating of most of the above-mentioned people with that name is far from certain, there is at least one who might date earlier (nos. 2) than the *treasurer Snb-sw-m-ꜥ(.j)*. For this official it is possible to propose that he is identical with the later *treasurer*. Many of the people with the name *Snb-sw-m-ꜥ(.j)* can be directly linked to the *treasurer* (nos. 3, 10, 11, 12). Some can be dated later (nos. 16, 18). It is obvious that a number of people are named after their master in whose household or administration they worked. It might therefore be possible that the name *Snb-sw-m-ꜥ(.j)* was so popular in the 13th Dynasty simply because of the *treasurer*. If this is the case it is another sign that *Snb-sw-m-ꜥ(.j)* was a person of exceptional power and influence.

It is also possible to confirm or exclude identifications through titles. Two people with the name *Snb-sw-m-ꜥ(.j)* bear the titles *zẖꜣw n ẖnrt wr* and *wr mḏw Šmꜥw*. Both titles are rarely found on documents relating to *treasurers*, whereas the title *high steward* is quite often connected with this office (Leiden 34 with a *treasurer* and three *high stewards* on it; on St. Petersburg, Hermitage 1084 both titles appear together; *Mkt-Rꜥw* [Grajetzki 2000: 45-46, no. II.2] bears both titles). It therefore seems more plausible to identify the *high steward* with the *treasurer Snb-sw-m-ꜥ(.j)*, than to link the other two people with him. However, a definitive proof for the identity of the *treasurer* with the *high steward*, in the form of a biographical inscription or a stela with the family of the *high steward* and the *treasurer* on it, is yet to be found.

The identity of *Snbj* is less problematic. Although on his monuments a full filiation is not always given and the name *Snbj* is particularly widely attested in the 13th Dynasty, there seems to be little doubt that all occurrences of a *treasurer Snbj* refer to the same person. In all cases where the filiation is given, the same mother (*nbt pr Tw-n.j*) and the same father (*ꜥnḫ n nwt Nb-pw-[Ptḥ]*) are always mentioned. Other people recorded on stelae of *Snbj* are datable with confidence to his time.

Of course the same problems of identification associated with the *treasurers* arise again with the other officials mentioned on their stelae and the stelae connected with them. Here, the identity of persons is often even more problematic. While it can be proposed that at a given time there was only one *treasurer* at the court, it is highly likely and indeed in some cases it can be proven that there were several people with titles such as *rḫ-njswt* or *jrj-ꜥt*. So long as there are no serious reasons against an identification, it has been assumed as a working hypothesis that people with the same name and identical or similar titles are one and the same person. However, one should avoid going too far on the basis of such unproven identifications.

Chapter 2
The *treasurers* and their staff in the 11th Dynasty and the 12th Dynasty before Senusret III

The first person datable to the 11th Dynasty with the title *treasurer* (*jmj-r3 ḫtmt*) is *Ṯtj* (Blackman 1931), known from a stela now in London (BM 614)(for earlier *treasurers* see the discussions in Fischer 1996: 50-52, Grajetzki 2000: 66, 72). The stela contains a long biographical inscription, which starts with the Horus name of Antef II (Wah-ankh). *Ṯtj*'s successor in the office of the *treasurer* might have been a person called *Bbj*, who is known from the stela New York MMA 14.2.7 (Hayes 1953: 153, fig. 61). The stela belongs not to the *treasurer* himself, but to the *overseer of the doors* (*jmj-r3 sb3w*) *M3ᶜt*, who might have been an official who served under the *treasurer*. Hayes dates *Bbj* to the reign of Mentuhotep II (Hayes 1953: 153).

Shortly before the reunification of Egypt under Mentuhotep II, a certain *Ḫtjj* became *treasurer* (Allen 1996a: 3-8). *Ḫtjj* is known from several sources. He is mentioned in the temple of king Mentuhotep II at Deir el-Bahari (Allen 1996a: 7, n. 22) and he had a huge tomb at Deir el-Bahari (Hayes 1953: 163-164; Allen 1996a: 5). *Ḫtjj* is also mentioned together with the king and his family in the rock inscriptions at Shatt er-Rigal (Petrie 1888: pl. XV, 443, pl. XVI, 489). *Ḫtjj* might have played an important part in the sed festival of the king, seeing that he is shown in the king's temple at Deir el-Bahari in scenes which are connected with the sed festival (Allen 1996a: 6).

Allen has brought to my attention another *treasurer* with the name *Jpj* who is known to him from the fragments of a wooden coffin from a private collection, which he saw on display in the Virginia Museum of Fine Arts (John Deaton is going to publish them; parts of the coffin are published in a sale catalogue: Writing & Lettering in Antiquity 16 (1994), no. 20). The titles on the coffin are: *ḫtmtj-bjtj, smr-wᶜtj, jmj-r3 ḫtmt, rḫ-njswt, jmj-r3 pr, sḏm sḏmt [wᶜ]* and *ḫtmtj-bjtj smr-wᶜtj, jmj-r3 ḥwt-[wrt 6], zḫ3w zm3t*. Like *Mkt-Rᶜw*, *Jpj* bears the title *steward* and *treasurer*. He may be identical with another *Jpj*, who is known from a Theban tomb and who was *vizier* (Grajetzki 2000: 12, no. 14). No other *treasurer* can be dated securely to the reign of Amenemhat I. A *treasurer* named *Rᶜjj*, known from the Reisner Papyri, has no ranking titles and might belong to the local administration and not to the highest court officials (Simpson 1986: pl. 24, G.1).

Mkt-Rᶜw (Grajetzki 2000: 45-46, no. II.2) was the successor of *Ḫtjj*. He bears the titles *high steward* and *treasurer*. His tomb, like that of *Ḫtjj* is extensively destroyed, so that little evidence for further titles has survived (Hayes 1953: 166-167). *Mkt-Rᶜw* is also mentioned as *treasurer* in the temple of Mentuhotep II at Deir el-Bahari (Naville 1910: pl. IX). He started his career as a common sealer (*ḫtmw*). This title is recorded in a rock inscription (Petrie 1888: pl. VIII, no. 213; Allen 1996a: 8, n. 61) which is dated to the forty-first year of Mentuhotep II. Important light is shed on the title by the tomb of the *jmj-r3 st W3ḥ*, who was buried in front of the tomb of *Mkt-Rᶜw* (Hayes 1953: 303-305). In the Late Middle Kingdom the title *jmj-r3 st*, which *W3ḥ* bears, is always very closely connected with the *treasurers*. The example of *W3ḥ* suggests that in the late 11th or early 12th Dynasty this title may already have been closely connected with the office of the *treasurer*. In the tomb of *W3ḥ* a large inscribed silver scarab was also found (Martin 1971: no. 390). The inscription mentioned *W3ḥ* with his title and *Mkt-Rᶜw* with *jrj-pᶜt* as his only title. *Mkt-Rᶜw* might have lived until the reign of Amenemhat I, but it seems that he died at Thebes, because he was in all likelihood buried in his Theban tomb (Arnold 1991a: 21-22). After *Mkt-Rᶜw* a certain *Jnj-jtj.f* might have been in office. He has a separate burial chamber in the same tomb as *Mkt-Rᶜw*, which is almost equal in size to the one of *Mkt-Rᶜw* (Arnold 1991a: 19, fig. 22). The exact position of *Jnj-jtj.f* is unknown. He might have been a relative of *Mkt-Rᶜw*, who was a *treasurer* at the court for some time after *Mkt-Rᶜw*.

Two *treasurers* are securely attested under Senusret I: *Sbk-ḥtp* and *Mnṯw-ḥtp* (Franke, Doss. 262). *Sbk-ḥtp* is mentioned together with an *jmj-z3*... in a painted rock inscription found at Hatnub (Posener 1968: pl. IX). The inscription is dated to the 22nd year of Senusret I. This date is important, because it gives a *terminus post quem* for the famous *Mnṯw-ḥtp* 's period of office as *treasurer*. From *Mnṯw-ḥtp* several monuments have survived but none of them are connected with subordinates working for him. On his famous stela in the Cairo Museum (CG 20539) he bears the *vizier's* titles and he is therefore often called *vizier* in Egyptological literature, but he might only have been a titular-*vizier*: that is to say a person promoted to the rank of *vizier* but not occupying the office (for discussion: Grajetzki 2000:

217-219). His tomb occupies a prominent site next to the pyramid of king Senusret I and has its own causeway. This seems to point strongly to the importance of its owner (Arnold 1991b). The size of the tomb is even more impressive when compared with the tomb of the *vizier Jnj-jtj.f-jqr* who lived slightly earlier, and who was buried inside the enclosure-wall of the pyramid complex of Amenemhat I (Franke, Doss. 146; the tomb: Gautier/Jéquier 1902: figs. 115-121). *Mnṯw-ḥtp* is not attested under Amenemhat II (Fay 1993).

There are three *treasurers* recorded from the reign of Amenemhat II. From the surviving records it is not possible to reconstruct the sequence of their succession. *Mrjj-k3w* (Mathieu 1998: fig. 1) is known from an inscription found in the Eastern desert with the name of Amenemhat II on it. *Rḥw-r-ḏr.sn* is known from an Abydos stela and from his tomb in Lisht (Hayes 1953: 177); the stela is datable by style to the reign of Amenemhat II (New York MMA 12.182.1; Hayes 1953: 333, fig. 221; for the dating Freed 1996: 328). Like *Mnṯw-ḥtp Z3-3st* (Simpson 1988) bears the title *vizier*. He might be the last in this sequence - he is buried in Dahshur, while *Rḥw-r-ḏr.sn* from the first part of the reign of Amenemhat II had his tomb at Lisht, as Dahshur had not yet been fully established as necropolis. The tomb of *Z3-3st* which de Morgan excavated and published must have been a most impressive monument. In the 19th century, Lepsius called it a pyramid (Simpson 1988: 57). The four relief slabs which de Morgan retrieved from the tomb belong among the highest quality private relief of the Middle Kingdom. His tomb chamber was decorated with Pyramid Texts (Allen 1950: 34-35). This is a feature of decoration which is sometimes found in Middle Kingdom tombs, but was not very common (compare the list in Willems 1988: 19-34). The *treasurer Sbk-m-ḥ3t* is only attested as *treasurer* by the fragments of an offering table found in his tomb next to the pyramid of Senusret III in Dahshur. The main titles on the few other published fragments from this tomb belong to the titles of the *vizier* (*treasurer* - de Morgan 1895: 33, fig. 64; *vizier* - 33, figs. 66-67). It seems therefore that *Sbk-m-ḥ3t* was promoted from the post of *treasurer* to that of *vizier*. *Sn-ʿnḫ* (de Morgan 1894: 86, no. 20) is known from a rock inscription at Sehel, where he reports the renewal of the channel *beautiful are the ways of Kha-kau-Re*. The inscription is dated to the 8th year of Senusret III. The *treasurer Zj-nj-Wsrt* dates to year 10 of an unspecified king on a papyrus which mentions the delivery of products from officials (Griffith 1898: pl. XV, XLIV.1). Beside the *treasurer* a *wḥmw n ʿrjjt* and a *ṯsw* are also mentioned on the papyrus. The date of the papyrus is not certain; it may come from the reign of Senusret III, Amenemhat III or even Amenemhat IV. The appearance of a *treasurer* at Lahun along with these officials might be related in some way to the building activities attested in this area in the late 12th Dynasty (Quirke 1990: 170-171).

The evidence for *Jjj-ḫr-nfrt* (Franke, Doss. 27) and the people working for him is substantial. Several stelae belong to him, to his family and to his subordinates. However, it should be pointed out that all the attestations for *Jjj-ḫr-nfrt* come only from these seven stelae, which must belong to his chapel in Abydos. The location of his tomb is not known. One would expect it to be in Dahshur or Lisht. The titles of the people depicted on the stelae with *Jjj-ḫr-nfrt* are already very similar to the titles found in the mid-13th Dynasty in connection with the *treasurers*, though there are some differences. Stela Cairo CG 20140 is dated to year one of Amenemhat III. On the stela are mentioned two *jrjw-ʿt wnwt* (Berlev 1978: 253-254, Berlev interprets the title as two titles: *jrjw-ʿt* and *wnwtj*) and two *jrjw-ʿt pr-ʿ3*. On stela Cairo CG 20310 a simple *jrj-ʿt*, is mentioned as well as a *ḫr-ʿ n jmj-r3 ḫtmt* (for *ḫrj-ʿ n jmj-r3 ḫtmt*) and a *jmj-r3 w*. On Cairo CG 20038 a priest, a *jmj-r3 st* and a *wdpw* are mentioned in addition. The title *jmj-r3 st* has already been noted above in connection with the *treasurer Mkt-Rʿw* and it will be shown that it was also very important in the administration of the *treasurers* in the 13th Dynasty. On stela London BM 202 and on Berlin 1204 two different people are mentioned with the title *rḫ-njswt*, a title which is also later attested very often in connection with the *treasurer*.

The stelae around the *treasurer Jjj-ḫr-nfrt* provide the earliest attestations for many titles which are typical for the administration of the *treasurers* of the 13th Dynasty (*wdpw*, *rḫ-njswt*). Some other titles also known from the administration under the *treasurers* in the 13th Dynasty (*jrj-ʿt n ʿḥ*, *jrj-ʿt wdpw*, *wdpw n ʿt*) appear for the first time on various monuments from the reign of Senusret III and Amenemhat III, though they are not yet directly linked with the *treasurers*.

The corpus of the Sinai inscriptions includes one item of special interest. It mentions a *treasurer* whose name is lost (Gardiner/Peet/Černy 1955: 90-91, no. 83, may also be from *Jjj-ḫr-nfrt* because in both this inscription, Sinai no. 83, and on stela Berlin 1204 an *jdnw n jmj-r3 ḫtmt Jmnjj[-snb]* appears). The titles of the people connected with the *treasurer* here are of great importance:

ḫtmtj-nṯr jmj-r3 ᶜḫnwtj wr n pr-ḥḏ
jdnw n jmj-r3 ḫtmt
jdnw ...
ᶜw
jmj-r3 ᶜḫnwtj n pr-ḥḏ
jmj-r3 z3 n ḫrtj-nṯr
jj...
ḫrtj-nṯr

There can be no doubt that these people were working for the *treasurer* in Sinai. All these titles are quite common in the Late Middle Kingdom, but are not very often found linked with the office of *treasurer*. Especially in the 13th Dynasty there is good evidence for the administration under the *treasurers*, including many different titles relating to their administration, but there is almost no evidence for the above-mentioned titles. In particular, the connection with the treasury (*pr-ḥḏ*) is not explicit in the 13th Dynasty sources. In the 12th Dynasty, several *treasurers* bear the title *overseer of the double treasury*, and *overseer of the double gold house* (*jmj-r3 prwj-ḥḏ, jmj-r3 prwj-nbw*) (Hayes 1953: 333, fig. 221; Cairo CG 20539; Berlin 1204). Both titles seem to disappear at the end of the 12th Dynasty, and are used not as function titles but only in longer title strings. In the late 12th Dynasty the titles *jmj-r3 ᶜḫnwtj wr n pr-ḥḏ* and *jmj-r3 ᶜḫnwtj n pr-ḥḏ* appear instead. Both of these new titles are only very rarely found in direct connection with the *treasurer*. One example for such a link is the above-mentioned inscription, while another example is stela Zagreb no. 8. The latter stela belongs to officials serving under a *treasurer*. The connection between the *treasurers* and the treasury therefore remains very unclear especially in the Late Middle Kingdom.

From the inscriptions found in Sinai, several titles are known, which must belong to the administration under the *treasurer*. The titles found in these inscriptions are also well-attested in other sources such as stelae and statues. However, the titles known from Sinai are only very rarely associated with the *treasurer* on monuments outside of Sinai. The Sinai inscriptions reflect a special branch of administration, which is evidently not documented on other monuments. This circumstance shows very clearly how selective our sources are. The stelae and monuments which will be described in the following chapters might also have been set up in very specific circumstances. The officials mentioned on these monuments may represent a special part of the Late Middle Kingdom administration under the *treasurer*. Clearly, it may be only a part of that administration, while other parts are not mentioned on surviving monuments or may not even have been recorded at all and so are totally lost. Finally it should be mentioned that there are several titles combined with the title *treasurer* (*jmj-r3 ḫtmt*), like *scribe of the treasurer* (*zḫ3w n jmj-r3 ḫtmt*) or *deputy of the treasurer* (*jdnw n jmj-r3 ḫtmt*). All of these people clearly worked in the administration of the *treasurer*, but they are not often found on monuments connected with the *treasurer*.

Chapter 3
Treasurers and their administration at the end of the 12th Dynasty and in the early 13th Dynasty

The evidence for *treasurers* and their administration from the end of the 12th Dynasty to the mid 13th Dynasty is not very substantial, but shows that structures similar to those already known under *Jjj-ḫr-nfrt* continued. The appearance of the seals with administrative titles in this period is of greatest importance. Seals are very common for *treasurers*, particularly in the 13th Dynasty and in the Second Intermediate Period. The *treasurer Ḥ3r*, for example, is the non-royal person with by far the highest number of surviving seals in all of Egyptian history (Martin 1971: nos. 984-1088a; Martin 1979: nos. 73-74, further attestations: Ryholt 1997: 60. n. 172). The dates for the first administrative seals with the titles and names of officials are not secure, but there is a person dated under a king Senusret who might already have a scarab seal (Martin 1971: no. 234; Cairo CG 20181; Grajetzki 2000: 189-190, no. XII.11: *jmj-r3 bjtjw Jnj-jtj.f*). The scarab seal of *W3ḥ* (Martin 1971: no. 390. pl. 47A), which dates to the beginning of the 12th Dynasty, is not typical. The inscriptions are on the back: it might have been some kind of amulet with the name of the owner on it. The underside of the scarab is not decorated with an inscription, but with spirals and the hieroglyphic signs 'nefer' and 'ankh'. The dating of individual scarabs of the Late Middle Kingdom is not easy. Martin (1971: 6) places his backtype no. 3 in the late 12th Dynasty. At least one seal of a *treasurer* has this backtype (Martin 1971: no. 1111, from Abydos). It belongs to the *ḥrj-sšt3 pr-njswt ḫtmtj-bjtj jmj-r3 ḫtmt Ḥrw*. None of the other *treasurers* who might date to the same time are attested on seals (Grajetzki 2000: 54-55, nos. II.14-17).

The first *treasurers* who are known from seals and from other monuments are very hard to date. At the moment it is not possible to say more than that they may belong to the end of the 12th or to the beginning of the 13th Dynasty. From *Snb.f* (stela Florence 2500, Bosticco 1959: nos. 30a,b; Martin 1971: no. 1606; Martin reads: *Snb.tjfj*) a stela with an offering table is known as well as one seal. The identification of the seal-owner with the stela-owner is not very secure because this name is so common.

From *Ḥrfw*, who is known securely from a magnificent felspar weight (Petrie 1926: pls. VII, XL, no. 4355) and less certainly from a block statue (James 1974: 49 (111), pl. XXXVI, compare Grajetzki 2000: 55, no. II.18) two seals are attested (Martin 1971: nos. 1142-1143). It is not possible to date him more precisely than late 12th Dynasty to early 13th Dynasty.

Some *treasurers* who are only attested on seals can be placed in the first half of the 13th Dynasty, because they use the bee-hieroglyph in the writing of *ḫtmtj-bjtj*. The bee was replaced in the second half of the 13th Dynasty by the red crown (Grajetzki 1995). The following *treasurers* exclusively use a bee in the writing of *ḫtmtj-bjtj* and are only attested on seals. They might therefore date to the early 13th Dynasty:

(ᶜḏ)-Zḥwj (Martin 1971: nos. 388, 1629; Martin 1979: no. 55)

Wpw-m-ḥꜣb (Martin 1971: no. 407)

Ḥrw(Martin 1971: no. 1111)

Ḫntj-ḫtjj-m-zꜣ.f Snb is known from a high quality statue, said to come from Abusir (Cairo CG 408), and from a stela found at Harageh or Lahun (Copenhagen ÆIN 1539, Jørgensen 1996: 196-197, no. 82 with following entry museum number in error). Several officials with other titles appear on his stela. The stela is decorated on two sides. On one side an *jrj-ᶜt n jmjw-ḥꜣt* is mentioned, who is simply called *jrj-ᶜt* on the other side of the stela. The same person is also called *his child* (*ẖrd.f*) in connection with the *treasurer*. Although the dating of *Ḫntj-ḫtjj-m-zꜣ.f Snb* is not certain, this might be one of the first attestations of the phrase *ẖrd.f* (list of attestations: Franke 1983a: 305-306). The title *jrj-ᶜt n jmjw-ḥꜣt* is only known from this monument. Berlev (1978: 237-238) translates it as *Chamberlain of the ancestors*, which he thinks is connected with the context of the stela, which was placed in a necropolis. Also mentioned on the stela is an *jmj-rꜣ ᶜẖnwtj wr n jmj-rꜣ ḫtmt.*

On the stela of *Snb.f* (Florence 2500, Bosticco 1959: nos. 30a,b) which is also decorated on two sides, an *jrj-ᶜt wdpw* is mentioned. The *jrj-ᶜt wdpw* is described as *ẖnms.f -his friend* (on the expression *ẖnms*: see Franke 1983a: 355-359). The title combination *jrj-ᶜt wdpw* is very common in the mid 13th Dynasty. Here the title is found linked with a *treasurer* for the first time. The exact dating of *Snb.f* is not certain and one may argue that he is even later than the mid 13th Dynasty. As well as the *jrj-ᶜt wdpw* who is mentioned on the stela there are also an *ᶜftj* and the *nbt pr Jbj* who is the mother of the *jrj-ᶜt wdpw*. The stela was therefore evidently commissioned by the *jrj-ᶜt wdpw* for himself and for his mother.

The end of the 12th Dynasty or the beginning of the 13th Dynasty seems the most plausible date for one or more *treasurers* with the name *Jmnjj* (Reisner 1923: 524-525, no. 47; Adam 1959: 214-215; without preserved ranking titles: Petrie 1902: pl. LX.3). Their sequence and even their number are not known. One of them is the owner of a huge sarcophagus found in Tanis, which must have originally come from Hawara (Montet 1947: 81-82, pl. XLVII), since the offering formula mentions *Osiris, the lord of the land of the lake.* A date for this person under Amenemhat III (who was buried at Hawara) or a little bit later therefore seems quite secure. A treasurer named *Jmnjj-snb* may be dated to about the same time, or to the early 13th Dynasty (Petrie 1925: pl. XXVIII). A treasurer *Ḫpr-kꜣ* dates to the 13th Dynasty (Turin Cat. 3064; Franke, forthcoming).

Chapter 4
Snb-sw-m-ᶜ(.j)

(Franke, Doss. 666, 667; Franke 1988; Franke 1994: 65-66; Grajetzki 2000: 57-59, no. II.22)

Snb-sw-m-ᶜ(.j) is the first *treasurer* after *Jjj-ḫr-nfrt* who is relatively well dated. Since many monuments are known from *Snb-sw-m-ᶜ(.j)* it seems highly likely that he stayed in office for a quite long time. His monuments can be divided into several categories. Of particular importance are the stelae from Abydos, which were in most cases set up by members of his staff. Apart from the stelae numerous seals are known from the *treasurer*. Other monuments mentioning *Snb-sw-m-ᶜ(.j)* are all from the Fayum-Memphis area. There is a bronze statue which most likely comes from Hawara, several papyri fragments from Lahun mentioning him and an inscription fragment with religious texts recorded at Dahshur. Some monuments mention a *high steward Snb-sw-m-ᶜ(.j)*. As argued above, he may be identical with the *treasurer*.

In the following lists all the monuments which relate to the *treasurers Snb-sw-m-ᶜ(.j)* and *Snbj* have been collected. First monuments referring directly to the *treasurers* will be mentioned and then there follows a list of monuments mentioning people related to the two *treasurers*. After many of the names a dossier (Franke 1984) has been added for further reference and for the relative dating of the stela to other stelae. People collected in a dossier by Franke but marked here with a ?, are not considered further because the relationship of the monuments put together in the dossier seems too uncertain. For people not yet collected in a dossier but known from other documents, the references to their other monuments are given. The measurements and the provenance of each stela - where known - are given after the museum number. In general only men with titles are mentioned.

Monuments of *Snb-sw-m-ᶜ(.j)* as *high steward*

1. Cairo CG 20075 (81 x 49 cm), unprovenanced
   Main person (left): *ḥrj-wḏb Zj-nj-Wsrt*
   Main person (right): *jrj-pᶜt, ḥ3tj-ᶜ, ḫtmtj-bjtj, jmj-r3 pr wr Snb-sw-m-ᶜ(.j)*
   The titles and name of *Snb-sw-m-ᶜ(.j)* are also included in the offering formula, which frames the stela. *Snb-sw-m-ᶜ(.j)* is therefore clearly the main owner of the monument.
   Other people mentioned on the stela are:

   jmj-r3 ᶜḫnwtj ḫrp sk Jjj-jb
   jmj-r3 ᶜḫnwtj Kmtw
   jmj-r3 gnwtjw Snb
   jrj-ᶜt wb3 Jmnw-m-ḥ3t
   jrj-ᶜt n ᶜḥ Snb (? Franke, Doss. 610)
   Wpw-w3jwt-ḥtp (the father of *Snb-sw-m-ᶜ(.j)*)
   ḫrj-ḥ3b ḥrj-tp n Ḥrj-šj.f Snb...
   ḫrj-ḥ3b zḫ3w spḫrw Snb-ᶜnḫ
   zḫ3w wr n sḏmw Z3-Stjt
   zḫ3w mḏ3t Jjj-ᶜḏ (Franke, Doss. 21)
   smwjj ḥrj-tp n Sbk Šdjt Tḫw

The family of the *high steward* is shown in the first register of the stela. His father *Wpw-w3jwt-ḥtp* is sitting on the right side under his son. His mother *Srwḫ-jb* is sitting in front of her husband *Wpw-w3jwt-ḥtp*. In the following registers appear officials belonging to the palace (*jrj-ᶜt, jrj-ᶜt n ᶜḥ*), officials in charge of building projects (*jmj-r3 ᶜḫnwtj ḫrp sk*) and people with religious titles (*ḫrj-ḥ3b*).

The appearance of the title *zḫ3w wr n sḏmw* (*chief scribe of the one who hears*) which is also recorded on stelae Cairo CG 20087 and CG 20562 requires further comment. The title is not very common, but both stelae also belong to a *high steward*. In general, it therefore seems that the *zḫ3w wr n sḏmw* was closely connected with the *high steward*. It was presumably a scribe working for him or *the overseer of the sealers* (who also appears on Cairo CG 20087). The common suffix titles *sḏmw rmṯ* and *sḏmw šnᶜw* of the *overseer of the sealers* should also be mentioned. The *overseer of the sealers* was another official quite closely connected with the *high steward* (Grajetzki 2000: 115). The *zḫ3w wr n sḏmw* was therefore a scribe working for the *high steward* or *overseer of the sealers* in their juridical positions.

It shows further the juridical aspect common to these two officials. The title is not *scribe of the high steward* or *scribe of the overseer of sealers*. This may show that the *zẖꜣw wr n sḏmw* would be fixed not to one specific official or office but to at least two or more officials in a specific position or function.

List of the title holders

zẖꜣw wr n sḏmw 

Jp-ꜥnẖw	Martin 1971: no. 120
Nb-pw	Cairo CG 20562 (shortly before Neferhotep I)
Ḥrw-nẖt	Turin inv. Cat. 1613 (Amenemhat III ?, see appendix II)
Zꜣ-Stjtt	Cairo CG 20075 (Neferhotep I or earlier)
Ptḥ-Nmtj	Cairo CG 20087 (13th Dynasty)

zẖꜣw wr (n) sḏmw rmṯ 

Jjj-mrw	Berlin 7288 (late 13th Dynasty, see appendix III)
Jmnjj	Paris, Louvre C 249 (late 12th Dynasty?)
Ḥr-wsr	Martin 1971: no. 1117 (no hieroglyphs are given, for the correct reading compare Franke 1982: 51)

zẖꜣw wr n sḏmw šnꜥw

ꜥꜣ-...	pBoulaq 18 XVII.2 (compare Quirke 1990: 98, n.1)

zẖꜣw wr n sḏmw rmṯ [wꜥrt] mḥtt

H̱ntj-ẖtjj(?)-m-zꜣ.f	Turin inv. Cat. 1613 (Amenemhat III ?, see appendix II; the reading of the title on the stela is not certain, compare Fischer 1997: 74-75, no. 1369).

2. Cairo CG 20459 (59 x 49 cm) Abydos, 'nördliche Nekropole'
   Main person: *ẖtmtj-bjtj, jmj-rꜣ pr wr Snb-sw-m-ꜥ(.j)*
   Under the chair of *Snb-sw-m-ꜥ(.j)* stands a dwarf with the name *Jmnw-m-ḥꜣt-snb.*

Cairo CG 20459 is a rectangular stela. The uppermost part is destroyed. The two wedjat eyes, a shen ring, three water lines and two jackals are still visible with a short inscription.
Snb-sw-m-ꜥ(.j) is sitting in the centre of the stela, wearing a long garment with an elaborate detailed upper border. In front of him there is an offering table and a mat with two vessels for ointment and two sacks for eye-paint on it. Under the chair there is a hes-vase and a set of washing dishes.

Cairo CG 20459 belongs to a small group of 13th Dynasty stelae which show the owner alone. They were most probably commissioned by the main person on them, while most other stelae of this date show the main person surrounded by his colleagues or his family. These stelae are sometimes of rather crude workmanship, while the stelae showing only one person alone are in general higher quality works of art (Bourriau 1988: 63). It is highly likely that these were the main stelae of Abydos chapels. However, they are not so common as to indicate that every chapel had such a stela. A family stela as the focus point of a chapel must have been the rule, while stelae mentioning one person alone are the exceptions. Stelae mentioning only one person are also attested in the sanctuary of Heqaib on Elephantine. A distinction may be necessary between stelae at the burial-place and stelae in offering-chapels or temples. A stela which comes from a place other than Abydos or Elephantine and mentions only one person or only a small family might be a tombstone; see for example the stela of the priest *Ḥrw-m-ẖꜥw.f* from Hierakonpolis, which was found in the courtyard of his tomb (Hayes 1947; Hayes 1953: 346-347) or several stelae of the late 13th Dynasty found at Thebes (Hayes 1953: fig. 227) or at Esna (Downes 1974: 67-83).

Stela Cairo CG 20459 might come from the same workshop (Simpson 1974: 4, n. 25) as Cairo CG 20075. Both stelae share the same richness of details: see for example the elaborate hair of the figures on the stela or the "floating" cup under the offering table.

3. Statue Leiden 1963/8.32
discussed in Franke 1988.

4. Seal Martin 1971: no. 1512 (the inscription is only published in transcription, as it was then in the Michaelides collection)

Group 1: Stelae mentioning the *treasurer Snb-sw-m-ʿ(.j)*

1.1. Leiden 14 (57 x 33 cm)

Snb-sw-m-ʿ(.j) (*ẖtmtj-bjtj, smr-wʿtj, jmj-rꜣ ẖtmt*) is sitting in front of an offering table. In front of him stands the *jtj-nṯr n Jtmw nb Jwnw Kkj*, who holds two round pots.

Other Titleholders:
jmj-rꜣ pr N-mnt-jb-sn
jmj-rꜣ ẖtmtjw Hr-nfr (Doss. 408)
jmj-rꜣ zꜣ n jkwjj (Ward 1982: no. 329) *Kkj*

The stela was commissioned by the *jtj-nṯr n Jtmw Kkj* and his family is dominant on it. His mother (*mwt.f nbt-pr Ḥr-m-ḥꜣb*) is sitting on the right, facing the *treasurer*. There is also a person called *his sister* and a person called *his daughter*. Since *his mother* clearly refers to *Kkj*, one may suppose that this is also true for both other references. However, the relationship between the people on the stela is not really clear.

1.2. London BM 215 (48.3 x 27.9 cm)
(letters after the name refer to the drawing of the stela; names without a letter appear in the vertical lines at the bottom of the stela)

Titles of *Snb-sw-m-ʿ(.j)* (A):
ẖtmtj-bjtj, jmj-rꜣ ẖtmt
Offering bearer: *jmj-rꜣ st Jꜣn* (B)
Other people :
jrj-ʿt n zꜣ n pr jmj-rꜣ ẖtmt ʿnḫ-rn (D)(?Doss. 184)
ḥrj-pr n pr-ʿꜣ Jjj-m-ḥtp (E)
ḥrj-pr n pr-ʿꜣ Zꜣ-Gbw (C)
zẖꜣw qdt (ẖrj-ḥꜣb) Zꜣ-Sbk (F) (Doss. 544. For the title combination see Franke 1994: 105)

The names and titles in the vertical lines at the bottom of the stela are not all clearly visible:
ḥrj-pr n pr-ʿꜣ Jtj
ẖrj-ḥꜣb dwꜣ-nṯr Rn-snb
ꜣṯw ... Ḏḥwtj

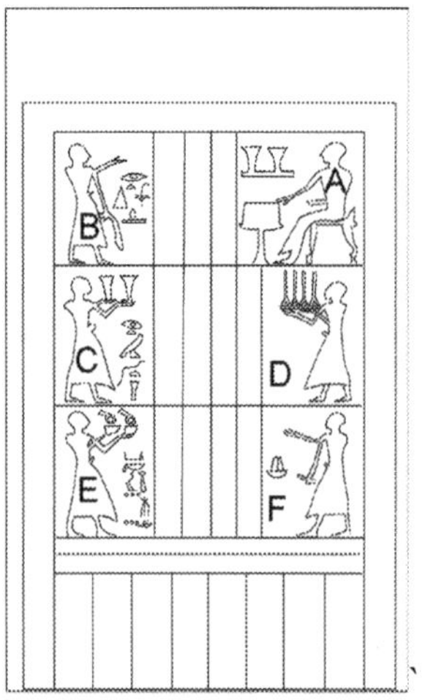

The monument belongs to a group of stelae showing the owner receiving offerings of eye paint, oils and cloth. On stela London BM 215 three people are shown offering these objects (C, D, E). Oils (C) and cloth (D) are in particularly typical of the offering lists and frises d`objets on the coffins of the 11th and 12th Dynasty. In the late 12th Dynasty both cease to be common on them. However, the same objects appear again later on the unique coffin of the *ḫrj-ḥ3b ḥrj-tp Ssnb-n.f* (Gautier/Jéquier 1902: 76-77, figs. 95-96, pls. XVI-XXV) of the 13th Dynasty. *Ssnb-n.f* might have been more or less contemporary with *Snb-sw-m-ᶜ(.j)* (Allen 1996b: 1, 6). The objects painted on his coffins are almost identical with the offerings made to *Snb-sw-m-ᶜ(.j)* (garments, oil, eye paint). These things therefore still seem to be the most important objects for a funerary ritual in the 13th Dynasty.

These offerings were already very important for elite burials in the Old Kingdom. Pyramid Text spells 50 - 57 which are concerned with offering oil to the dead were written in the inside of a coffin at the head (Willems 1988: 212-213). In the 13th Dynasty, religious texts on coffins are no longer found to the same extent. However the customs and rituals for which the oils were used went on, and therefore it sometimes happens, that people offering oils are depicted on stelae (Berlin 7732, Cairo CG 20147, CG 20556, Leiden 15), even though the normal offering is food and drink on the offering table. People offering oil are also known from stela Berlin 7311, which belongs to *Rḥw-ᶜnḫ*. However, in general this kind of stela is not very common; there are more examples that show some vessels for ointment next to the offering table (Cairo CG 20016, CG 20017, CG 20435). There are a few examples of one person with several stelae where on one of the stelae food offerings are made, while on the other ointment offerings are given. The stelae Cairo CG 20015, CG 20101 and CG 20562 belong to the *high steward Jmnjj*. On Cairo CG 20015 he is shown sitting in front of a rich food offering table. On Cairo CG 20562 he is sitting with a tomb-chapel behind him, in front of a table with three ointment jars. Finally, on the third stela (Cairo CG 20101) he is sitting under a pavilion, again in front of a rich offering table with food on it. A similar arrangement is found on the stelae of the *overseer of the beer chamber Snpw* (ANOC 55). On Berlin 7309 *Snpw* is sitting in front of an offering table and on stela Toulouse 1181 he is sitting in front of ointment jars. Stela New York MMA 69.30 1 might have been part of a similar set of stelae. The stela belongs to the *z3b r3-Nḫn ᶜnj*. He is depicted with his wife. In front of them are two figures: a *wᶜb n Ḥwt-Ḥrw nbt Jwnt*, who is offering a jar of ointment and a kneeling woman who is offering two sacks of eye paint. The offering formula on the stela mentions *ᶜntjw*. This seems not to be very common in the 13th Dynasty, when *snṯr* is more popular.

1.3. London BM 252 (61 x 49.5 cm)
On the left side at the top *Snb-sw-m-ᶜ(.j)* is shown standing. He is holding a *sekhem* sceptre and a long staff.
Titles of *Snb-sw-m-ᶜ(.j):*
jrj-pᶜt, ḥ3tj-ᶜ, ḫtmtj-bjtj, smr-wᶜtj, jmj-r3 ḫtmt
Offering man (standing just in front of the *treasurer*): *jmj-r3 st Rnpt*
Other figures: *šmsw n ḥq3 Ddw* (? Doss. 768)

Next to these men, three women (*Jpw, Jtj* and *Pwpt*) are mentioned with the title *nbt-pr*. *Jtj* is also known from other stelae of the *jmj-r3 st Rnpt*, but the relationship between the two is never made explicit. She might be his mother or his wife.

The stela might have been set up by the *jmj-r3 st Rnpt* for himself and his family.

1.4. Cairo CG 20334 (42.5 x 26 cm) Abydos, 'nördliche Nekropole'
Snb-sw-m-ᶜ(.j) is sitting on the right. His titles: *ḫtmtj-bjtj jmj-r3 ḫtmt*
Offering man: *jmj-r3 st n ḫntj Znb*
jrj-ᶜt wᶜb Ḥkkw
wdpw Jjj
wdpw Snb (? Doss. 625)
wᶜb n Jtmw P3-ntj-nj
wᶜb n 3st-jrt Snb.tjfj
wᶜb (?) 3st-jrt Snpw
ḫrj-ᶜ ....
wᶜb n Ḥwt-Ḥrw nbt Jwnt Z3ḥj

zj n dpwt-ˁȝt Kmtw (he might be the same person as the man mentioned on Pittsburgh Acc.2983-6701 as *šmsw)*
nfw S(n)ˁˁ-jb
šmsw Sbk-ḥtp
ḥrj-pr …snt

In the roundel of the stela are the two wedjat eyes, the shen ring and two jackals. The tails of the jackals hang down into the field with the inscriptions. The stela is executed in the silhouette style (pp. 62-63). On the whole, the workmanship seems to be a little bit careless, see for example the writing of "t" instead of "r" in the title *jmj-rȝ ḫtmt*. The monument is similar in style and iconography to stela London BM 215 and it should be noted that the execution in relief of the main figure is almost identical.

1.5. Cairo CG 20718 Abydos, 'nördliche Nekropole'
Snb-sw-m-ˁ(.j) (only title: *jmj-rȝ ḫtmt*) is shown sitting on the left in front of an offering table. On the right stands the *jrj-ˁt wdpw Ppj* (Doss. 236), who is called *his beloved son* and '*born of Pzš* '.

jrj-ˁt wdpw n ˁt dqr Rn-snb (? very common name, Doss. 366)
jrj-ˁt wdpw Nb-jrwt (Doss. 287)
jrj-ˁt wdpw Nn-ḫ<m>.sn (? Doss. 86)
jrj-ˁt wdpw Ḫnms (Doss. 460)
jrj-ˁt wdpw Sbk-ḥr-ḥȝb (Doss. 570)
jrj-ˁt wdpw Sbk-ḥr-rkḥj
jrj-ˁt wdpw Sbk-ḥtp (Doss. 583)
jrj-ˁt wdpw Snb
jrj-ḫr… Jtȝ
wdpw ˁq Rn-snb (Doss. 365)
zḫȝw n ḫntj Ptḥ-wr
zḫȝw n ḫntj Mm

The stela is discussed in Berlev 1978: 275

1.6. Pittsburgh Acc.2983-6701 (54 x 36 cm)
Snb-sw-m-ˁ(.j) is shown sitting on the left in front of a richly laden offering table. In the offering formula, he is called: *jmj-rȝ ḫtmt Snb-sw-m-ˁ(.j).*
The *jmj-rȝ st n jmj-rȝ ḫtmt Rnpjj.f* is shown standing on the right and behind him the *nbt pr Jtj.*
Other people:
ˁb…
wbȝ (?) Jȝ-m-ˁnḫ
wdpw Jȝw-m-nwt (this man is also mentioned on Dublin UC 1360; Chicago, Field Museum of Natural History no. 31647 and on stela Roanne 163)
Ptḥ-ḥtp
nfw Jw.j-rrjjj
Snb-sw-m-ˁ(.j)
šmsw Kmtw (compare Cairo CG 20334)
(for style compare comments on Dublin UC 1360; p. 21. no. 2.2)

1.7. St. Petersburg, Hermitage 1084 (67 x 38 cm)
people:
jmj-rȝ ˁḫnwtj ḥrp sk Ḫmj
jmj-rȝ ˁḫnwtj ḥrp sk Sbk-ḥtp (Doss. 591)
jmj-rȝ pr n ḥmt-njswt Sˁȝw
rḫ-njswt Snn (Doss. 682)
ḫtmtj-bjtj jmj-rȝ pr wr Snbj-šrj
ḫtmtj-bjtj smr-wˁtj jmj-rȝ ḫtmt Snb-sw-m-ˁ(.j)
ẖrd.f ḫtmtj-nṯr Rdj-n.f-n.j
ẖrd.f Snb

The figure of the main person on the stela has its hands raised in adoration of Min-Hor-nakht. From the inscriptions it is not clear which name belongs to the main person. Although *Snb-sw-m-ᶜ(.j)* is the person with the highest titles, he is not mentioned in the offering formula. In the offering formula *Sbk-ḥtp* is the beneficiary. He might therefore be the person who commissioned the production of the stela. It is also not easy to find parallels for the style of the monument. The main figure and the figure of Min are worked with many details. These include most notably, the hair, the elaborate design of the upper part of the garment and the feather crown of Min (a similar garment is found on Turin inv. Cat. 1620; Cairo CG 20459, London 1367=Hall/Lambert 1912: pl. 28; all these examples date to about the time of Sobekhotep III - Neferhotep I). However, the shapes of the figures and hieroglyphs are not very well executed; in places the hieroglyphs are awkwardly arranged, so that there are even problems reading them.
The stela belongs to the offering table Marseilles no. 252: both must once have formed a unit (following Franke, mentioned in Bolshakov/Quirke 1999: 53).

1.8. Roanne 163 (51 cm in height)
Main person: *ẖtmtj-bjtj, smr-wᶜtj, jmj-r3 ẖtmt Snb-sw-m-ᶜ(.j)*
Man making offering: *jmj-r3 st n jmj-r3 ẖtmt Ḥrj-w3ḥ*
Main person in the second register: *jmj-r3 st n jmj-r3 ẖtmt Ḥrj-w3ḥ*
Three men are making offerings before *Ḥrj-w3ḥ* in the second register:
jmj-r3 pr n sẖt Nṯr-pn-nb.j
wdpw ... J3w-m-nwt (Gabolde 1990: 36 – 'le préposé pur au petit bétail')
wdpw Snb-sw-m-ᶜ(.j)
Other figures:
ḥrj-ᶜ n wdpw n ᶜt jwf Nfr-tm (he may also appear on Zagreb no. 8)
wb3 n ᶜt-ḥnqt Wr-n-ḥq3

In the roundel of the stela are the two wedjat eyes, the shen ring and at the far ends of both sides an east and a west sign with an offering arm. The stela is almost identical to Zagreb no. 8 in style and layout. Both stelae were presumably commissioned at about the same time (pp. 64-65).

1.9. Turin Cat. Suppl. 1298 (unpublished and included here from museum visit notes; the surface of the stela is in part heavily eroded)
Main person: *ẖtmtj-bjtj, smr-wᶜtj, jmj-r3 ẖtmt Snb-sw-m-ᶜ(.j)*
Offering man: *ḥrj-pr n pr-ᶜ3 (?)*
Other people (all other names are destroyed or not readable from the position in the display):
ḥrj-pr n pr-ᶜ3 Ḫntj-ḫtjj-ḥtp
ḥrj-pr n pr-ᶜ3 Ḫntj-ḫtjj-ḥtp
The roundel and layout of the stela are similar to stela Roanne 163.

2. Papyri
Snb-sw-m-ᶜ(.j) is mentioned on three papyrus fragments found at Lahun, which are now in the Petrie Museum, University College London. To judge from the size of the signs and the spacing between the lines, the fragments seem to be the remains of large format papyrus sheets. They might have once all belonged to one big scroll. Other fragments in the Petrie Museum might also belong to this manuscript series. In the following section, only those three fragments on which the name of *Snb-sw-m-ᶜ(.j)* appears are discussed. The forthcoming publication of all Lahun accounts papyri will provide the full context.

UC 32104 (plate 7)
... the *jmj-r3 ẖtmt Snb-sw-m-ᶜ(.j)*
... one cow, given to the stable of this town.
... one goose, given to the stable (?) ...
...100, given to the district (?) of the overseer ...

The delivery of animals and fowl in low numbers seems to be unusual for the papyri. On the other fragments which do not mention the name or title of *Snb-sw-m-ᶜ(.j)*, fish is the principal commodity mentioned.

UC 32104 (plate 7)
... deliveries ...
... *smr-wᶜtj, jmj-r3 ẖtmt* ...
... fisher...
...
...

UC 32100 (plate 8)
This fragment is too damaged to give even a sketch of a translation. Mention is made of the titles *wḥmw* and *ᶜnḫ-sẖtj* and some other people (*Wsr-Mnṯw*). The sense of the contents of the fragment is unclear. The verso of the fragment is important, because it preserves dating to year four of an unnamed king.

It is hard to say why *Snb-sw-m-ᶜ(.j)* stayed in Lahun. The *treasurer Zj-nj-Wsrt* (Griffith 1898: pls. XV, XLIV.1) of the 12th Dynasty can be connected with some royal building activity which was organised from this town. It seems that *Snb-sw-m-ᶜ(.j)* collected food, which was allocated to the local stables/warehouses. While on the surviving fragments with the name of the *treasurer* mention is made of animals, the other fragments include accounts of fish. Once, the Fayum Lake (*šj-Sbk*) is mentioned. Lahun might still have been the administrative centre for the Fayum in the middle of the 13th Dynasty. The food production of the area which was delivered to the palace and court might have been collected here before it was brought to the residence. Of all places in the Fayum Lahun is closest to the residence at Lisht by river. However, this explanation of the appearance of a *treasurer* at Lahun is little more than a guess. It should also be mentioned that one seal of *Snb-sw-m-ᶜ(.j)* was found at that site.

3. Seals (Martin 1971: 534-535, 1513-1541a, Vodoz 1978: 148-149, no. 90; Martin 1979: no. 43; Bourriau 1988: 159)
Snb-sw-m-ᶜ(.j) is the first treasurer with a huge series of scarab seals. In general, it seems that in the late 12th Dynasty and early 13th Dynasty a person had one or only a few seals. For later *treasurers* many seals are attested. *Snb-sw-m-ᶜ(.j)* is the only *treasurer* with many seals who is datable. Unfortunately most of these are unprovenanced, but one of the seals was found in Lahun (Martin 1971: no. 1517) and another in Lisht (op. cit. no. 1526).
Two versions of the title string can be found on the seals:

1. *Ḫtmtj-bjtj, jmj-r3 ẖtmt* (Martin 1971: nos. 1513-1514; Quirke/Fitton 1997: 427, 437, n. 67). All three seals have features which separate them from the following group of seals. No. 1514 has a different "backtype" and uses the red crown instead of the bee in the writing of *ẖtmtj-bjtj*. No. 1513 and BM EA 69522 (op. cit. Quirke/Fitton 1997) are decorated with spirals.

2. *Ḫtmtj-bjtj, smr-wᶜtj, jmj-r3 ẖtmt* (Martin 1971: nos. 534, 535, 1515-1541a; Martin 1979: no. 43). Although this group of seals is quite consistent, always using the same titles and the same writings, it is possible to divide the seals into types, according to the arrangement of signs.

Type 1 (Martin 1971: nos. 34-535). The reading of the titles and name on the seals starts at the top, goes down the right and then up the left. The ʿ in the writing of the name has a stroke, which is not attested on any of the other scarabs.

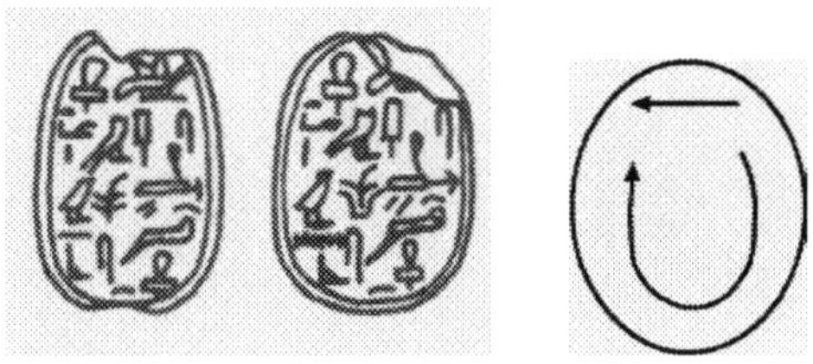

Type 2 (Martin 1971: nos. 1527-1529). The *wʿ*-sign in the writing of *smr-wʿtj* is oriented in the opposite direction. *Wʿtj* is written without *tj*.

Type 3 (Martin 1971: nos.1516, 1520, 1524). *Wʿtj* is again written without *tj* and is placed in the middle of the scarab. *Ḫtmtj* in *ḫtmtj-bjtj* is written without a *t*.

Type 4 (Martin 1971: nos.1517-1519, 1524, 1526). The most common writing.

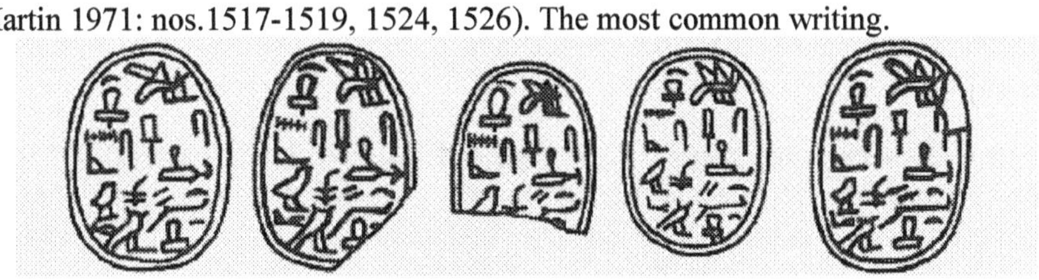

Type 5 (Martin 1971: nos. 1516, 1535), base type 3d (Martin 1971: pl. 49).

Type 6 (Martin 1971: nos. 1521, 1536, 1533). Similar to type 4, but the ᶜ is written before the *m*. On two of the seals, *smr-wᶜtj* is written without *tj*.

All other seals: They all show some small typical features which makes it not very useful to divide further into sub-groups.

These groups of scarab seals are internally so similar, always using the same orthography and the same arrangement of signs, that one may wonder if each group was made in a workshop by a craftsman or by several craftsmen using the same prototype ('Vorlage'). The types which are only attested once might be produced as single scarabs unless the other examples of these types are simply missing. Nevertheless, this shows clearly that scarabs were produced in large numbers, at least for some officials.

4. The tomb

Mariette found an object inscribed with the name and title of *Snb-sw-m-ᶜ(.j)* in Dahshur. Mariette 1889: 583 describes it as: "Fac-simile d´un croquis sur une feuille isolé". It seems therefore that Mariette copied this inscription at Dahshur. He failed to mention on what kind of object the text was written. It was most probably a stone block. If it really was a stone fragment it is highly likely that it came from a tomb and this would mean that even in the 13th Dynasty, tombs could be decorated with long religious texts. Elsewhere the custom of decorating stone parts of a tomb with religious texts is attested in Hawara, where Petrie found a fragment with a religious text, which mentioned a *high steward* (with pyramid spells 21; 13-14; Petrie 1889: pl. VI, no. 13). The fragment might date under Amenemhat III and might come from the tomb of a *high steward* who was buried next to the pyramid of Amenemhat III. An alabaster slab/stela with religious texts was also found in the tomb of king Hor of the 13th Dynasty (de Morgan 1895: 94, fig. 217), providing further evidence for the occurrence of such texts in a 13th Dynasty elite tomb on objects other than the coffin.

It seems less likely that the fragment once belonged to a wooden coffin. The preservation conditions for wood are not very good in Dahshur. Coffins with long religious texts are not very common in the 13th Dynasty, and the hieroglyphs on this kind of object are always mutilated, whereas the hieroglyphs on the *Snb-sw-m-ᶜ(.j)* fragment are complete. There are some attestations in the 13th Dynasty for religious texts on statues, stelae and shrines. In the final analysis, the fragment might perhaps belong to such an object (Franke 1994: 241-251), though a stone slab still seems the most plausible material.

The fragment in question bears 15 columns and one horizontal line of inscriptions. The horizontal line gives the name and titles (*jrj-pᶜt, ḥ3tj-ᶜ, ḫtmtj-bjtj, smr-wᶜtj, jmj-r3 ḫtmt*) of *Snb-sw-m-ᶜ(.j)*. The columns bear the coffin text spells 723 and 67 (Franke 1983a: 24). Spell 67 is otherwise attested on three coffins from Thebes (T1C, T2C, T9C), on a coffin from Saqqara (Sq3C) and on a coffin from el-Bersheh (B10C). Spell 723 has only one parallel in el-Bersheh (B3Bo), but the version of *Snb-sw-m-ᶜ(.j)* is much longer with a substantial insertion. On coffin T2C (from Thebes) the beginning of the spell survives, but the main parts are lost. This coffin is of particular importance here because it is the only other source where both spells (67 and 723) occur, albeit with each spell on a different part of the coffin. There are finally some sources from the 18th Dynasty for the spell CT 723 (pBM 10819; TT29 compare Kahl 1999: 156-157). All the coffins discussed are datable to the Early Middle Kingdom (Willems 1988: 70-72, 105, 106, 112-114), and some might even date to the 11th Dynasty. Only B10C belongs to the early 12th Dynasty (Willems 1988: 74-75). However CT 723 is still used in the 18th Dynasty, so that the copy of *Snb-sw-m-ᶜ(.j)* occupies some kind of middle position.

Summary: *Snb-sw-m-ᶜ(.j)*

Date:
None of the monuments of *Snb-sw-m-ᶜ(.j)* is dated to a specific king, and sadly also not one of the subordinates directly connected to him is dated by a king's name. *Snb-sw-m-ᶜ(.j)* must have been in office before the *treasurer Snbj*, who is securely dated under Neferhotep I and Sobekhotep IV. The careers of some officials clearly show the succession of the two officials.

The *jrj-ᶜt wdpw Ḫnms* appears together with *Snb-sw-m-ᶜ(.j)* on stela Cairo CG 20718. On stela Cairo CG 20614 he has been appointed in the meantime to the post of *rḫ-njswt*. On this stela the *treasurer Snbj* appears. The *rḫ-njswt Snn* should also be mentioned. On stela St. Petersburg Hermitage 1084 he is shown together with *Snb-sw-m-ᶜ(.j)*, while on Cairo CG 20614 he appears together with the *treasurer Snbj*. However, the *jmj-r3 ᶜḫnwtj n Ḏd-b3w Nnj* is most important for the dating of *Snb-sw-m-ᶜ(.j)*. *Nnj* appears on stela Cairo CG 20023. This stela is datable under the *treasurer* through people, who appear on it and on stelae of the *treasurer* (most important: *Nb-jrwt*, Franke, Doss. 287). The *jmj-r3 ᶜḫnwtj n Ḏd-b3w Nnj* is also mentioned on stela Cairo CG 20391. This stela belongs to the *high steward ᶜ3b-m-ᶜ(.j)*, who is datable under Sobekhotep II (Grajetzki 2000: 89, III.17, via pBoulaq 18 where he is mentioned).

The first visible stage of his career is as *high steward*. Several monuments can be assigned to him. The *high steward Snb-sw-m-ᶜ(.j)* was the son of a certain man called *Wpw-w3jwt-ḥtp* and a woman with the name *Srwḫ-jb*. His mother *Srwḫ-jb* was the daughter of a woman *Jjz-nbw Mnw-wn*. A person with the title and name *zḫ3w md3t Jjj-ᶜḏ* was the brother of *Snb-sw-m-ᶜ(.j)*'s mother (the family is briefly discussed in Franke 1983a: 23-24). He is depicted on the stela of the *high steward Snb-sw-m-ᶜ(.j)* (Cairo CG 20075) behind him and is also known from a stela of his own (Cairo CG 20072), where he bears no title. The latter stela is a rather poor monument which might reflect the quite low position of its owner. Although the position of *Snb-sw-m-ᶜ(.j)*'s father is not known, it seems to be quite obvious that *Snb-sw-m-ᶜ(.j)* comes from a relatively humble social background.

From the position of *high steward* he might have been directly appointed as *treasurer*. It should be pointed out that the identity of these two people is still not proven and that there are no people attested on the monuments of the *high steward* who appear on monuments of the *treasurer*. As *treasurer*, *Snb-sw-m-ᶜ(.j)* was one of the most important figures of the 13th Dynasty. The exact date of his time in office is still a problem, but his career might already have started before Sobekhotep II. While *Snbj* is definitely the successor of *Snb-sw-m-ᶜ(.j)*, and is dated under king Neferhotep I and with a high degree of probability under Sobekhotep IV, there remain problems in pinpointing the date of *Snb-sw-m-ᶜ(.j)*. His time in office might span most of the reign of Neferhotep I, if *Snbj* started his career right at the end of his reign. Equally, it is possible that *Snbj* was promoted to *treasurer* at the beginning of the reign of Neferhotep I. In this case *Snb-sw-m-ᶜ(.j)* might have been in office before Neferhotep I (Franke 1994: 66). Finally, the possibility that Neferhotep I and Sobekhotep IV reigned for some time in a coregency should be mentioned (Ryholt 1997: 227-228). The period of office of *Snb-sw-m-ᶜ(.j)* might therefore even have lasted into the reign of Sobekhotep IV.

No wife or children of *Snb-sw-m-ᶜ(.j)* are known. On stela Cairo CG 20718 there is a person (*Ppj*) with the title *jrj-ᶜt wdpw*, and he is called *his beloved son*. At the moment it is not possible to decide if he was a real son of *Snb-sw-m-ᶜ(.j)* or a person working in the administration of the *treasurer*. No details about his work in office are known. The high number of stelae set up for him makes it highly likely that he was involved in building activities in Abydos. Whether this was under king Khendjer or under Neferhotep I can only be guessed. He built a tomb for himself in Dahshur where he was most probably buried.

Group 2: stelae on which the main person is somebody mentioned as second person on stelae of group 1

2.2. Dublin UC 1360 (height: 52.5 cm)
Main person: *jmj-r3 st n jmj-r3 ḫtmt Rnpjj.f* (the offering man on stela Pittsburgh Acc.2983-6701)
offering man: *wdpw J3w-m-nwt*
jmj-r3 st jwf Sbk-nj-pw
other persons:

jmj-r3 st n ᶜt ḫnqt Nb-swmnw
jmj-r3 st n ᶜt tʾ Jmnw-m-ḥ3t
jmj-r3 st n ᶜt tʾ ᶜ3mw Snb
jmj-r3 šnᶜw n wḥ3t W3ḥ
jrj-ᶜt n ... ᶜnḫw
jrj-ᶜt n Kpnj Snb.tjfj
wdpw n ᶜt ... r

The stela is almost identical in style and layout to Pittsburgh Acc.2983-6701. Both stelae might have been produced at about the same time by the same craftsmen.

2.3. Zagreb no. 8 (58 x 29 cm)
Main person: *jrj-ᶜt ᶜ3mw Ḥrj-w3ḥ* (the offering man on stela Roanne 163)
Offering men: *wdpw Nfr-tm, wdpw Snb-sw-m-ᶜ(.j)*
Other people mentioned:
jmj-r3 ᶜḫnwtj n pr-ḥḏ Ḥḏr
jrj-ᶜt n ᶜḥ Snfrw (the father of *Ḥrj-w3ḥ*)
ᶜftj Wr-n-ḥq3
mḏḥw n ᶜt šnᶜw Jmnjj

Group 3. Stelae on which people are mentioned who are already known from Group 1, but who were not in the second position on group 1 stelae.

3.1. Cairo CG 20023 (52 x 23 cm) Abydos, 'nördliche Nekropole'
Main person: *ḫtmtj-bjtj, jmj-r3 ḫtmtjw, jmj-jz, ᶜnk.f*
Offering man: *zḫ3w n ḫntj Ḫwjj*
Other people mentioned:
jmj-r3 ᶜḫnwtj n Ḏd-b3w Jwjj
jmj-r3 ᶜḫnwtj n Ḏd-b3w Nnj (Franke, Doss. 330)
jmj-r3 ᶜḫnwtj ḫrp sk Snpw (Franke, Doss. 598)
jmj-r3 st n ᶜt jwf (?) Rn-snb (? Franke, Doss. 371)
jmj-r3 st Nb-jrwt (Franke, Doss. 287)
jmj-r3 dpwt Jqr
jmj-ḫntj Rn-snb
jrj-ᶜt jwf(?) Wr-nb (Franke, Doss. 212)
jrj-ᶜt jwf(?) Snb.f
ᶜw Rn-snb
ḫtmw n ᶜt jwf Zr (Franke, Doss. 683)
zḫ3w wdḥw Mnw
zḫ3w pr ᶜnḫ Kkw (Franke, Doss. 725)
zḫ3w n ḫntj Rn-snb (Franke, Doss. 362)
zḫ3w n ḫntj Jjj (Franke, Doss. 6)
zḫ3w n ḫntj Jbj
zḫ3w n ḫntj Nfr-tm
zḫ3w n ḫntj Ḫwjj
zḫ3w n ḫntj Ttj (Franke, Doss. 735)
zḫ3w ḏ3ḏ3t Jbj
swnw Jmnjj (not *wr swnw* - see Ghalioungui 1983: 24)
ṯ3w n ḫft-ḥr Ptḥ-wr (Franke, Doss. 241)
ṯ3w n ḫft-ḥr Mwt

The stela is of special interest, since it is datable under Sobekhotep II. See the discussion of the dating of *Snb-sw-m-ᶜ(.j)*.

3.2. Cairo CG 20616 (44 x 30 cm) Abydos, 'nördliche Nekropole'
Main person: *ḫtmtj-bjtj, jmj-r3 ḫtmtjw, šmsw njswt Ḥr-nfr* (Franke, Doss. 408; he also appears on stela Leiden 14)
Other people mentioned:

jmj-rꜣ pr n ḥtp-nṯr H̱wj-rw
jmj-rꜣ st Snb(b)
wꜥb ꜥꜣ n Sbk-Šdjt ꜥnẖw
ḥrj-pr n pr-ꜥꜣ Nb-sẖwt
ḥrj-n ꜥt Rꜥw-ḥtp
ẖrd.f zꜣw-ḥnkt Hr-nfr

3.3. Cambridge Fitzwilliam Museum E 1.1840 (61.4 x 37.6 cm)
Main figures: *ẖtmtj-bjtj, jmj-rꜣ ẖtmtjw, šmsw njswt Tjtj* (Doss. 732; Grajetzki 2000: 89-90, no. III.18), *jrj-ꜥt wdpw H̱ntj-ḥtjj-ḥtp* (? Doss. 473)
Offering man in front of *Tjtj*: *jrj-ꜥt wdpw H̱nms* (Doss. 460: appears on CG 20718 with the same title)
Other people mentioned:
jrj-ꜥt wdpw Jtnjj (?)
jrj-ꜥt wdpw Sbk-ḥtp (?) (Doss. 583)
wdpw jrj-jꜥḥ Nb-jrwt (Doss. 287; *Nb-jrwt* also appears on CG 20718, but with the title *jrj-ꜥt wdpw*)
wdpw jrj-jꜥḥ Rn-snb (Doss. 364)
wdpw jrj-jꜥḥ Rn-snb (Doss. 364)
wdpw jrj-jꜥḥ Sbk-ḥr-ḥꜣb (Doss. 570)
wdpw jrj-jꜥḥ...
ḥrj-pr Sbk-ḥtp (? Doss. 586)
zẖꜣw pr ꜥnẖ Kkw (Doss. 725)
zẖꜣw n ẖntj Rn-snb (Doss. 362)
ṯꜣw n ẖft-ḥr Ptḥ-wr (Doss. 241)

Many of the people mentioned on the stela are also known from other stelae but with different titles. On this stela the title *wdpw jrj-jꜥḥ* appears quite often. The stela might have been set up during a special occasion on which the officials bore the title *wdpw jrj-jꜥḥ*.

3.4. London BM 238 (53.35 x 38.1 cm);
Main person: *rẖ-njswt H̱nms* (Franke, Doss. 460)
Offering man (without titles): *Jbj-jb* (he appears on Marseilles no. 223 as *jmj-rꜣ pr*)
Other people mentioned:
jmj-rꜣ ꜥẖnwtj ẖrp sk Sbk-ḥtp (Franke, Doss. 591)
jmj-rꜣ ꜥẖnwtj ẖrp sk Snb.f (Franke, Doss. 648)
zꜣw-ḥnkt Snb-sw-m-ꜥ(.j)
wdpw Sbk-nj-pw (? Franke, Doss. 564; he may also appear on Dublin UC 1360, with the title *jmj-rꜣ st jwf*)
zẖꜣw n ẖntj (?) Rz

For style of the stela compare Marseilles no. 223 (p. 24, no. 3.8)

3.5. Munich 36 (38 x 25 cm)
Main person: *jrj-ꜥt wdpw Sbk-ḥr-ḥꜣb* (Franke, Doss. 570)
Other people mentioned:
wdpw n ꜥt dqr Jw-snb
wdpw n ꜥt t’ ꜥn
wdpw n ꜥt t’ Snꜥꜥ-jb
jrj-ꜥt n šnꜥw Snbb.f
ꜥnẖ n nwt Snb.f

3.6. Vienna ÄS 182 (51 x 29.5 cm)
Main person: *jrj-ꜥt wdpw H̱nms* (Doss. 460)
Offering man: *ḥsj Ṯnj-ꜥꜣ (?)*
Other people mentioned:
jmj-rꜣ wꜥrt n zẖꜣww mwt-njswt Ḥkkw
jrj-ꜥt Jmnjj (? Franke, Doss. 78)
jrj-ꜥt Sbk-ḥr-ḥꜣb (Franke, Doss. 570)
wdpw n ꜥt t’ Snb.tjfj (Franke, Doss. 674)

3.7. London BM 903 (52 x 32 cm)
Main figures:
jmj-rꜣ st Ḫnms (Doss. 460)
jmj-rꜣ ḫtmtjw Nḫjj (Doss. 331, also mentioned on Leiden 34 but with the title *high steward*, London BM 903 is therefore earlier)
Offering man: *wdpw n ꜥt tꜣ Snb.tjfj*
Other people mentioned:
jrj-ꜥt n wršw Rdj
jrj... Ḫrw-b-nfr
wꜥb n Mnṯw Jmnw-m-ḥꜣt
wdpw n ꜥt jwf Jtj
wdpw n ꜥt tꜣ Jmnw-m-ḥꜣt (Doss. 78)
wdpw n ꜥt tꜣ(?) Ḥrj (?) (Doss. 423)
wdpw n ꜥt tꜣ (?) Ḥtpj
wdpw n ꜥt tꜣ Snb-jtw.f(?) (Doss. 674)
wdpw Ḥrj
ẖrd n kꜣp Ḥrj
ẖrd n kꜣp Sbk-ḥtp
zẖꜣw n ḫntj Kwjjt
šmsw Ḫmj (?)

3.8. Marseilles no. 223 (58x 43 cm) (Maspero 1890: 114. The published copies of the inscriptions are not always exact. The following titles are based on a museum photo)
Main person: *rḫ-njswt Ḫnms* (Doss. 460)
Other people:
rḫ-njswt Sbk-ḥr-ḥꜣb (Franke, Doss. 570)
jrj-ꜥt šnꜥw n Nbw-kꜣw-Rꜥw Wr-n(.j)-Ptḥ
ḥrj pr n pr-ꜥꜣ Jbj
jbḥw Kꜣmw
jrj-ꜥt šnꜥw n Sbk-nfrw Hbjj
jmj-rꜣ wꜥrt n nbwjj Ptḥ-wr
Nfr-ḥtp (Franke, Doss. 322)
jmj-rꜣ pr Jbj-jb (he also appears on London BM 238)

The stela is separated in two main parts. Under the roundel with two jackals on a shrine is the upper half, which is divided into two registers. In the first register sit mainly colleagues of *Ḫnms*. In the second register sit three women, a further colleague (*Ptḥ-wr*) and *Jbj-jb* who was the nephew of *Ḫnms*. In the lower half of the stela on the left sits *Ḫnms*. In front of him sit various members of his family. The stela is very similar in style and arrangement to London BM 238. Both were evidently commissioned and produced at the same time by the same craftsmen. Of special interest are the titles *jrj-ꜥt šnꜥw n Nbw-kꜣw-Rꜥw* and *jrj-ꜥt šnꜥw n Sbk-nfrw*, which seem to refer to the cult of king Amenemhat II and of the queen Sobeknofru. Both were still worshipped in the 13th Dynasty.

3.9. Turin inv. Cat. 1620 (47 x 39.5 cm)
Main person: *rḫ-njswt Ḫnms* (Doss. 460)
Other people (not shown as figures on the stela but listed with name and titles under *Ḫnms*):
jrj-ꜥḏ Jbw
ḥrj-pr n pr-ꜥꜣ Ḥrj
ꜥnḫ (n) ṯt ḥqꜣ Jjj
ꜥnḫ n nwt Ḥrj
ꜥnḫ n nwt Mnṯw-ḥtp
... Nb-jrwt

List of stelae and other monuments which can related directly to the above listed stelae. The monuments are mentioned first, followed by the person through whom the connection is possible and references to the relevant monuments treated above (for more see Franke's dossiers).

Cairo CG 20072 (*Jj-ꜥḏ* who also appears on Cairo CG 20075)

Cairo CG 20160	(*wdpw jrj-jꜥḥ Rn-snb, zẖꜣw n ẖntj Tjtj* on Cambridge Fitzwilliam Museum E 1.1840)
Cairo CG 20117	(*jmj-rꜣ st ... Rn-snb* on Cairo CG 20023, 20716)
Cairo CG 20286	(*zẖꜣw n ẖntj Ttj* on Cairo CG 20716, CG 20160 and 20023)
Cairo CG 20391	(*jmj-rꜣ ꜥẖnwtj n Ḏd-bꜣw Nnj* on Cairo CG 20023)
London BM 225	(*wdpw Snb* on Cairo CG 20334)
Stockholm NME 18	(? *wdpw Jmnw-m-ḥꜣt* on Vienna ÄS 182)
Tübingen 479	(*wdpw n ꜥt dqt - wdpw jrj-jꜥḥ Pzšw* on Cairo CG 20160)
Vienna ÄS 142	(*zẖꜣw n ẖntj Jjj* appears here and on Cairo CG 20023)
London BM 249	(*wdpw Tjtj* on Cambridge Fitzwilliam Museum E 1.1840 as *jmj-rꜣ ẖtmtjw*)
Vienna ÄS 143	(the *jmj-rꜣ ꜥẖnwtj n kꜣp* and *jmj-rꜣ ẖtmtjw Tjtj* appears here and on Cambridge Fitzwilliam Museum E 1.1840)

Chapter 5
Snbj

(Franke, Doss. 634; Grajetzki 2000: 56-57 [II.21])

Two stelae mentioning him as *rḫ-njswt*, presumably from the time before he was appointed *treasurer*.

1. Louvre C39
   Main person: *rḫ-njswt Snbj*
   Offering man (*ḫrd.f*): *wˁb ˁȝ n Sbk nb Šdjjt Wr-n.j-nṯr.j* (Doss. 211)
   Other people mentioned:
   jmj-rȝ gnwtjw Ḥr-nfr
   jrj-pḏt Rn-snb

2. Cairo CG 20225 (47 x 24 cm), Abydos, 'nördliche Nekropole'
   Main person: *rḫ-njswt Snbj*
   Offering man (*ḫrd.f mrjj.f*): *wdpw n ˁt ˁḏ? Nṯr.j-n(.j).m-ḏw*
   Other people mentioned:
   jmj-rȝ pr Wr-n(.j)-Ptḥ (he may also appear on Rio de Janeiro 646 [2436])
   jrj-ˁt n ˁḥ Rjs.fj

Group 1: Stelae mentioning *Snbj* as *treasurer*.

1.1. Cairo CG 20614 (52 x 32 cm), Abydos, 'nördliche Nekropole'

   Main figures:
   jrj-pˁt, ḥȝtj-ˁ, ḫtmtj-bjtj, smr-wˁtj, jmj-rȝ ḫtmt Snbj (sitting on the left)
   rḫ-njswt Snn (sitting on the right; Franke, Doss. 54)
   Other people mentioned:
   jmj-rȝ ˁḫnwtj n kȝp ˁnḫ.tjfj
   jmj-rȝ ˁḫnwtj n kȝp Snb (Franke, Doss. 628; Berlin 7311, Vienna ÄS 140, Wadi el-Hudi, 23, 24)
   jrj-wdpw (jrj-ˁt wdpw ?) Snb
   rḫ-njswt Jzj
   rḫ-njswt ˁwj
   rḫ-njswt Rn-snb
   rḫ-njswt Rn-snb-šrj
   rḫ-njswt Rḫw-ˁnḫ (Franke, Doss. 389)
   rḫ-njswt Ḫnms (Franke, Doss. 460)
   rḫ-njswt Kwkw
   ḫtmtj-bjtj, jmj-rȝ sḫtjw Jbj (Franke, Doss. 54; Leiden 33)
   ḫtmtj-bjtj, jmj-rȝ ḫtmtjw, jmj-jz Nṯr-m-mr

Many high officials appear on the stela. Some of these officials are already known in connection with *Snb-sw-m-ˁ(.j)* (*rḫw-njswt Ḫnms, Snn*). The stela might therefore date to the very beginning of *Snbj*'s time in office.

1.2. Leiden 34 (56 x 34 cm)

   Stela Leiden 34 is decorated on both sides.
   Side A:
   Main person: *ḫtmtj-bjtj, smr-wˁtj, jmj-rȝ ḫtmt Snbj*
   Other people mentioned:
   jtj-nṯr n Sbk Šdjtj Mnw (Franke, Doss. 250)
   jtj-nṯr n Sbk Šdjtj Nb-swmnw
   rḫ-njswt Sbk-ḫȝb
   ḫtmtj-bjtj, jmj-rȝ pr wr Nḥjj (Franke, Doss. 331)
   ḫtmtj-bjtj, jmj-rȝ pr wr Zȝ-jtjt
   ḫtmtj-bjtj, jmj-rȝ pr wr Zȝ-Stjt (Franke, Doss. 85)
   ḫtmtj-bjtj, jmj-rȝ [ḫtmtjw], sḏm šnˁw Nn-ḥm.sn

On side A, *Snbj* is sitting in front of an offering table. Above the table stands a vessel for ointment. In the next register stands the *jtj-nṯr n Sbk Šdjtj Mnw*. All other figures are depicted sitting on the ground in the two lower registers.

Side B:
Main person: *jtj-nṯr n Sbk Šdjtj Mnw* (Franke, Doss. 250)
Other people mentioned:
jtj-nṯr n Sbk Šdjtj Ptḥ-wr-b3w
ḥ3tj-ᶜ, jmj-r3 ḥwt-nṯr Z3-Sbk
ḥ3tj-ᶜ, jmj-r3 ḥwt-nṯr Zr (? Franke, Doss. 684)
jtj-nṯr n Sbk Šdjtj ᶜnḫ
ḫtmtj-bjtj, ḥm-nṯr Sbk Sbk...

On side B, the *jtj-nṯr n Sbk Šdjtj Mnw* is depicted sitting on a chair in front of an offering table. In the three registers under him all figures are shown sitting on the ground.

On the edge of the stela: *ḫtmtj-bjtj, ḥm-nṯr n Sbk Ḥq3-jtj*

The stela seems to have been commissioned by the *god's father of Sobek* named *Min*, who is mentioned on it twice. On one side (A) of the stela he is standing in the second position under the *treasurer Snbj*. People belonging to the court dominate this site of the stela. On the other side of the stela he is sitting on a chair as the main person. This side is dominated by people belonging to the local administration and local temples.

The stela might have been set up on the occasion of a visit by *Snbj* and some other courtiers to Shedit.

1.3. Vienna ÄS 140 (49.1 x 30.8 cm)
Main person: *ḫtmtj-bjtj, smr-wᶜtj, jmj-r3 ḫtmt Snbj*
Person in the second position: *rḫ-njswt Rḥw-ᶜnḫ* (Franke, Doss. 389)
Other people with titles:

jmj-r3 ᶜḫnwtj n k3p Snb (Franke, Doss. 628)
jmj-ḫt-z3w-pr Mbw
wdpw jrj-jᶜḥ Nḫjj
ḫrd.f wdpw n ᶜt t' N-mḥt-jb (Franke, Doss. 328)
šmsw šms Zrjj

The *rḫ-njswt Rḥw-ᶜnḫ* appears twice on the stela. In the upper register he is shown sitting on the ground in front of the *treasurer*. In the second register he occupies a position in the middle, while the *jmj-r3 ᶜḫnwtj n k3p Snb* is sitting on the ground at the left in the main position of this register. *Snb*'s cousin was the wife of *Rḥw-ᶜnḫ*. The people mentioned on the stela might therefore belong mainly to the family of the *rḫ-njswt Rḥw-ᶜnḫ* (Hein/Satzinger 1988: 4.57).

1.4. London BM 428 (90 x 34 cm), found in Abydos (Peet 1914: 111 - 'found face downward in wind-blown sand in north cemetery not far from the Shuneh')
In the first register of the stela Ptah is shown standing in a small shrine (left) and facing him, Amun-Re (right).
In the next register is *Snbj (jrj-pᶜt, ḥ3tj-ᶜ, ḫtmtj-bjtj, smr-wᶜtj, jmj-r3 ḫtmt)* sitting in front of an offering table and in front of him are three standing figures (*wr mḏw Šmᶜw Nfr-smn Ptḥ-ᶜḏ*; *jrj-pḏt Ḥtp*; *zḫ3w wdḥw Ptḥ-z3w-jb*).

Donor of the stela: *ḫrd.f zḫ3w wdḥw Ptḥ-z3w-jb*
Other people mentioned:
jmj-r3 šnᶜw Z3ḥj (father of the *zḫ3w ḥr ḫtmt Tjtj*)
jmj-r3 dpwt Jbj
jrj-ᶜt n Kpnj Sbk-ḥr-ḥ3b (? Franke, Doss. 570)
z3w-ḥnkt Jjj-ᶜnḫ (Franke, Doss. 14)

ꜥnḫ n nwt Nfr-rnpt
ꜥnḫ n nwt Sn-jw
ꜥnḫ n nwt Snb (? Franke, Doss. 624 - without filiation)
ꜥnḫ n nwt Ḏd.tw
zẖ3w ḥr ḫtmt Tjtj

In the Late Middle Kingdom it is not very common that two different gods are depicted on one stela, though there are already examples from the time of Amenemhat III/Amenemhat IV with two gods in a shrine in the roundel (Hall/Lambert/Scott-Moncrieff 1912: pl. 50). Another example is the stela of queen *Nbw-ḫꜥj.s* (Louvre C 13) which may date slightly later than the stela of *Snbj*.

This is the only stela from Abydos in the group discussed which comes from an excavation, but it was not recovered in its original context.

1.5. Liverpool no. M13661 (69.0 x 38.5 cm, limestone, unknown provenance, the stela was destroyed in the Second World War, 1941); pl. 1

Two standing figures are shown on the stela facing each other. The offering formula names the *rḫ-njswt Snn* as the main person, and he must therefore be the larger person standing on the left. The *ḫtmtj-bjtj, smr-wꜥtj, jmj-r3 ḫtmt Snbj* appears standing on the right. He is shown a little bit smaller but with the same long garment. The stela is not very well made. The text contains some orthographic mistakes: *rḫ-njswt* is written *ḫn-njswt*, and the word *sn* ‘they' is written once with two 'n's.

1.6. Liverpool no. M13635 (57 x 34 x 5 cm, limestone, unknown provenance, the stela was destroyed in the Second World War, 1941); pl. 2

Main person: *ḫtmtj-bjtj, smr-wꜥtj, jmj-r3 ḫtmt Snbj*
Person standing in front of him: *jmj-r3 ꜥẖnwtj, jmj-r3 t3-mḥw Jtjj*
Other men mentioned:
z3-njswt Ḫdr
jmj-st-ꜥt n Ptḥ rsj-jnb.f Jb
jmj-r3 st Nḫjj
ꜥnḫ n nwt Rn.f-ꜥnḫ
jmj-r3 dpwt Zkr
jmj-r3 ꜥẖnwtj, jmj-r3 t3-mḥw Wsr

Special mention must be made of the *z3-njswt Ḫdr*. The name *Ḫdr* seems otherwise only to be attested as a variant of the king's name Khendjer (Ryholt 1997: 220). *Ḫdr* is described on the Liverpool stela as born of the *z3t-njswt Z3t-Ḫntj-ḫtjj*, who is sitting in front of him. She herself is identified as born of the *ḫkrt-njswt N-qr-ḥrj-jb* (*No thunder is in (her) heart*). The title *king's son* is attested in the 13th Dynasty as a title for persons who are certainly not the son of a king (Franke 1983a: 308-309). The title *king's daughter* was normally considered as worn only by women who were really daughters of a king (Schmitz 1976: 251-252; Ward 1986: 46-56). The mother of *Z3t-Ḫntj-ḫtjj* has the title *ḫkrt-njswt.* This title is very common for wives of officials in the late 13th and 17th Dynasty (see discussion), but it is not often linked with women in close contact with the king. It therefore seems that the Liverpool stela is a source for the title *z3t-njswt* used by a woman who was not the daughter of a king. However, there are also other ways of interpreting this source:

1. The woman with the title *ḫkrt-njswt* died before her husband became king and was therefore never able to bear the title *king's wife*.
2. She was the lesser wife of a king. The title *ḫkrt-njswt* might have been given to her later, on a different occasion.
3. The woman was the daughter of a king or was married to a king's son. The title *z3t-njswt* of her daughter would in this case mean *granddaughter of a king* (note that there is no single word for granddaughter in ancient Egypt; compare Dodson/Janssen 1989: 136).
4. The *z3t-njswt Z3-Ḫntj-ḫtjj* was married to king Khendjer.
5. Nobody in this family was related to king Khendjer. The name of the *king's son* might just indicate that he was born under that king.

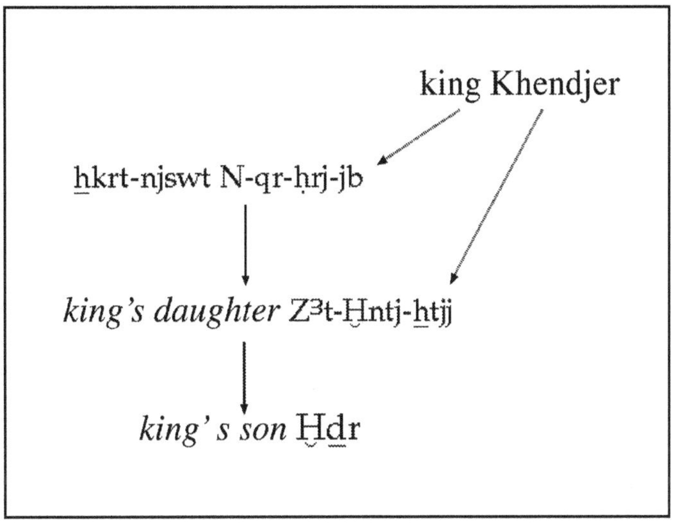

At present it does not seem possible to decide which explanation fits *N-qr-ḥrj-jb* best. There can be little doubt over the identity of the king to whom the family was related: king Khendjer, as the name is otherwise never attested. Naming a grandson of a king or a member of his family after the king is well-attested particularly in the 12th Dynasty (Amenemhat - Senusret - Amenemhat). For the 13th Dynasty evidence is lacking, since there is not much proof for grandsons and other members of the royal family. However, there are some examples of giving a grandson the name of his grandfather in the 13th Dynasty royal family (Ryholt 1997: 225, 321). Finally, the appearance of the *king's son Ḫd̠r* on a monument dating under king Neferhotep I/Sobekhotep IV throws some new light on the attitude of the kings of that period towards their predecessors. The memory of king Khendjer was evidently not avoided and even one of the highest officials of the time still remained in close contact with the family of the former king.

The two stelae in Liverpool come from the collection of Joseph Mayer, who bought many objects from several early 19th century collectors.

2. Rock inscription
De Morgan 1894: 87, no. 44, compare Habachi 1981: 78, fig. 4

Snbj is mentioned together with the family of king Neferhotep I (Habachi 1981): the *god's father Ḥꜣ-ꜥnḫ.f*, the *king's mother Kmj*, the *kings wife* (*Snb-sn*), three *king's sons* (*Zꜣ-Ḥꜣt-Ḥrw, Sbk-ḥtp, Ḥꜣ-ꜥnḫ.f*), and a *king's daughter* (*Kmj*). The *rḫ-njswt Nb-ꜥnḫ* is another official mentioned. *Snbj* takes the last position in the list. He has no ranking titles. One may argue that the inscription is a sign that *Snbj* visited the Aswan region (Franke 1994: 70). However several inscriptions from the *rḫ-njswt Nb-ꜥnḫ* are attested in this area (Grajetzki 2000: 93 III.25a-d), and it seems surprising that the *treasurer* is only once mentioned. Further it should kept in mind that *Nb-ʿnḫ* appears on stelae in the Heqaib sanctuary on Elephantine (Habachi 1985: nos. 44, 46); the *treasurer* does not appear there at all.

The situation seems to be quite similar to Abydos, where a *rḫ-njswt* set up a stela for a *treasurer*, as well as being mentioned on several stelae on his own, without the *treasurer*. The *rḫ-njswt Nb-ʿnḫ* is the active person, and might have really visited Aswan. This is supported by the fact that the *rḫ-njswt Nb-ʿnḫ* also set up monuments in the Heqaib sanctuary on Elephantine. The king and the *treasurer* are honoured by him, but need never have visited Aswan themselves.

3. Seals

Martin 1971: nos.1547-1556; Keel 1997: 112. no.22; Wegner 1998: 37, no. 24, fig. 19:8

The find place is known only for two seals. One seal comes from Tell el-ʿAjjul (near Gaza). Another (seal impression) is from the recently excavated mayoral palace at Abydos (Wegner op. cit.).

All the seals are of a similar design. Apart from the inscription, the base is undecorated. The writing of *ḫtmtj-bjtj* is always with a bee. There are two types of inscription on the base:

a. Name without seated man as determinative.

b. Name with seated man as determinative (Martin 1971: nos.1550-1552); one of the seals (no. 1550) omits the "t" in the writing of *smr-wʿtj* and *jmj-rȝ ḫtmt*.

Summary: *Snbj*

Date: *Snbj* is mentioned in a rock inscription (de Morgan 1894: 87, no. 44) together with the family of king Neferhotep I. The question is how long his period in office extended and whether it lasted into the reign of Sobekhotep IV. One of the officials of *Snbj*, the *rḫ-njswt Rḥw-ʿnḫ*, is dated to the 6th year of this king (in the rock inscription Wadi el Hudi no. 24). Therefore it may be supposed that *Snbj* remained in office under Sobekhotep IV.

The social background of *Snbj* is well known. His father was the *soldier of a town regiment Neb-pu* (*ʿnḫ n nwt Nb-pw*, Franke, Doss. 296; on the title: Berlev 1971). His mother was the *lady of the house Tuni* (*nbt pr T.w-n.j*). Kim Ryholt (1997: 298) pointed out that king Neferhotep I, whose father was also *ʿnḫ n nwt*, had the same social background. It therefore seems possible that the king appointed a person to his court whom he already knew from the time before he acceded to the throne. A further link to a royal family is the connection to the *king's son Khedjer*, who appears together with *Snbj* on stela Liverpool no. M13635. Although it is not possible to say anything concrete about this *king's son*, it is highly likely that he was a member of the royal family around king *Khendjer*. *Snbj* himself is first attested as *rḫ-njswt*. After that he was promoted, possibly by Neferhotep I himself, to the position of *treasurer*. He is attested on at least five stelae with this title; most of them must come from Abydos, but one of them perhaps comes from Medinet el-Fayum. *Snbj* is recorded in one rock-inscription near Sehel together with the family of king Neferhotep I. It is not clear whether he was really there, I have argued above that it is more likely that the inscription was only set up by one of his officials (*rḫ-njswt Nb-ʿnḫ*), who was on commission in this area. Nothing is known about *Snbj*'s burial place, his family or his other works.

Group 2: stelae and other monuments on which the main person is somebody who appeared as second person on a stela of the *treasurer*

2.1. Berlin 7311 (48 x 33.5 cm)
Main person: *rḫ-njswt Rḥw-ʿnḫ* (Franke, Doss. 389)
Two offering men: *wdpw n ʿt tʾ Snb.tjfj* (Franke, Doss. 674),
wdpw n ʿt tʾ N-mḥt-jb (Franke, Doss. 328)

Other people:
jmj-rꜣ ʿḫnwtj n kꜣp Snb (Franke, Doss. 628)
zꜣw-ḥnkt Jj-n-j
rḫ-njswt mꜣʿ Rn-snb
ḫrd.f wdpw n ʿt ḥnqt Sʿnḫ-Mnw
ḫrd.f Mrj-snb.f
wdpw n ʿt tʾ dqr Jr.wj-wn
wdpw n ʿt tʾ dqr Rn-snb (? very common name, Franke, Doss. 366)
At the bottom of the stela are two lines including the last phrases of "l'enseignement loyaliste" (Posener 1976: 49; Franke 1983a: 291, n.1).

2.2. Cairo CG 20104 (52 x 33 cm) Abydos, 'nördliche Nekropole'
Main person: *rḫ-njswt Rḥw-ʿnḫ* (Franke, Doss. 389)
Man making offerings: *jrj-ʿt wdpw n ʿt jwf Qqj* (Berlev 1978: 279 reads *Wnmj*)
Other people:

ꜣṯw ʿꜣ n nwt Nb-jtj
ꜣṯw ʿꜣ n nwt Ḫntj-ḥtp
jmj-rꜣ st Zꜣ-Gbw
jmj-ḫt-zꜣw-pr Nb-ꜣbḏw
jrj-ʿt nt mḏt Kꜣ.j-ʿnḫ
zꜣw-ḥnkt Jjj-ʿnḫ (Franke, Doss. 14)
wdpw Jtj-snb
wdpw n ʿt tʾ ʿnḫw (Franke, Doss. 171)
wdpw n ʿt tʾ Ptḥ-wr
wdpw Mnj
nḥmjjt nt nwt Rn.s-snb
ḥrj n tm N-jb
ḥrj-pr n pr-ʿꜣ Jꜣjj
ḥrj-pr n pr-ʿꜣ Wnw
ḥrj-pr n pr-ʿꜣ Ḥtpjj
ḥrj-pr n pr-ʿꜣ Ḫwjj
šmsw Jbj
nfw Nḫt

2.3. Cairo CG 20147 (48 x 34 cm) Abydos, 'nördliche Nekropole', the stela is heavily damaged in places
Two main figures: *rḫ-njswt Rḥw-ʿnḫ* (Franke, Doss. 389), *wdpw Nḫjj*
Man making offerings: *wdpw ʿq Rn-snb* (a person with this name and title appears three times on the stela; once called 'his son' *zꜣ.f* ; Franke, Doss. 365)
Other people:

jmj-rꜣ ʿḫnwtj n ṯꜣtj Mkmt
jrj-ʿt wdpw ...zꜣ
wdpw Nḫjj
ḥrj-pr n ... .-snb (Franke, Doss. 386)
zḫꜣw n ḫntj ... Jppj
[wdpw] ʿq Zꜣ-sj

2.4. Wadi el Hudi no. 24 (32 x 20 cm)
The stela is dated to year 6 of Sobekhotep IV
Main person: *rḫ-njswt Rḥw-ꜥnḫ* (Franke, Doss. 389)
Other person:
jmj-rꜣ ꜥḫnwtj n kꜣp Snb (Doss. 628)

2.5. Cairo CG 20282 (55 x 30 cm), Abydos, 'nördliche Nekropole'
The roundel of the stela contains two jackals on a shrine. The inscriptions identify them both as *Wepwawt, Lord of Abydos.*
Main person: *rḫ-njswt Snn* (also called *rḫ-njswt mꜣꜥ mrjj.f*)
On the right side the *zẖꜣw ꜥn njswt zmꜣjjt Mwt-wr* is depicted sitting.
Snn is shown sitting in front of an offering table (with only bread on it).
Other people:

jmj-rꜣ mrḥt Zꜣ-Sbk
ꜥnḫ n ṯt ḥqꜣ Zꜣ-Sbk
mḏḥ-njswt Rꜥj
mḏḥ-njswt Ḫntj-ḫtjj-ḥtp
ẖrd n kꜣp ꜥꜣb...
ẖrd n kꜣp Ptḥ-wr (or: *Zꜣ-Ptḥ)*
šmsw Snb.f
smsw hꜣjjt Snb.tjfj (zꜣ.f)

Group 3. Stelae on which people are mentioned, who are already known from Group 1, but do not appear in the second position.

3.1. Aswan Heqaib no. 47 (Franke 1994: 71-72) (89 x 46 cm)
Main figures:
jmj-rꜣ ꜥḫnwtj ẖrp kꜣt Ḫꜥ-kꜣw-Rꜥw-snb (Franke, Doss. 451)
ḥꜣtj-ꜥ jmj-rꜣ ḥmw-nṯr H̱nmw-ḥtp

Other people mentioned:
ꜣṯw (?) n w Ḫꜥ-kꜣw
jmj-rꜣ wꜥrt n gnwtjw Jrt-ꜥḏ
jmj-rꜣ wꜥrt n zẖꜣww qdwt Jw.f-nr-sn
jmj-rꜣ pr Wꜣḥ-kꜣ
jmj-rꜣ pr wr Nḥjj (Doss. 331)
jmj-rꜣ pr Nḥjj
jmj-rꜣ zꜣ Nmtj
ꜥnḫ n nwt Zj-nj-Wsrt
ẖtmw ẖr-ꜥ n jmj-rꜣ ẖtmt Snpw
ẖrtj-nṯr Sbk-ḥtp
ẖrd.f Ptḥ-wr
zẖꜣw ꜥt ḥnkt Ḫpr-kꜣ
zẖꜣw n pr-ḥd Snb (Doss. 611)
šmsw Zj-nj-Wsrt
šmsw Nb-ḥr

As on Leiden 34 there are local officials (in this case from Elephantine, though the only definite example is a *ḥꜣtj-ꜥ jmj-rꜣ ḥmw-nṯr*) together with officials from the residence mentioned on this stela.

3.2. Durham 1941 (75 x 42 cm)
Main person: *ḥꜣtj-ꜥ jmj-rꜣ ḥmw-nṯr Jmnw-m-ḥꜣt Zꜣ-Stjt* (Doss. 85=Grajetzki 2000: III.19, also mentioned on stela Leiden 34)
Offering men: *zꜣ.f mrjj.f ḥꜣtj-ꜥ jmj-rꜣ ḥmw-nṯr Wꜣḥ-kꜣ*
sn.f ḥm-nṯr n Rꜥw Snb.f

3.3. Leiden 33 (51 x 32 cm)

Main person: *ḫtmtj-bjtj jmj-r3 sḫtjw Jbw* (Doss. 54, also mentioned on stela CG 20614). Many members of the family of *Jbw* appear on the stela. The other people recorded on it mainly have titles which are in a broad sense connected with the military.

jmj-r3 st Snb.tjfj
jmj-z3 Z3-Gbw
jrj-ʿw Tjtj
ʿftj Sʿnḫ-Ptḥʿnḫ-sḫtj Ttj
ḥrj tm Bbj (Franke, Doss. 227. He also appears on Wadi el-Hudi no. 23, which might date under Sobekhotep IV; the connection to Bologna KS 1929 seems to be not very secure because of the common name and the common title but the stela shows some iconographical features which are typical for that time – p. 62)
ḥrj tm Nfr-tm
ḥrj tm Rrj
ḥrj tm Jpt
ḫrj-ʿ Nfrw
šmsw Jnd.f
šmsw Nʿ-dpwt ?
šmsw Ḫrj
šmsw ḥq3 Jtj

3.4. Moscow 5350 (43.5 x 31 cm)

Main person: *ḥ3tj-ʿ jmj-r3 ḥmw-nṯr n Šdjt Jmnw-m-ḥ3t Z3-Stjt* (Doss. 85, also mentioned on Leiden 34 but with the title *high steward*; Moscow 5350 is therefore earlier)

Offering person: *z3.f mrjj.f ḥ3tj-ʿ jmj-r3 ḥmw-nṯr W3ḥ-k3*

3.5. New York MMA 68.14 (39 cm height)

Main person: *jmj-r3 ḫtmtjw šmsw njswt Jzj* (also mentioned on CG 20614 but with the title *rḫ-njswt*, CG 20614 is therefore earlier: the identification is clear from the similar name of the mother: *B(w)j(w)*)

Offering person: *ḥrj n tm Rn-snb*

Other people:
sḫm-ʿ Ḫnmw-ḥtp
šmsw n ḥq3 Tjtj
šmsw Z3-Jmnw

All the people on this stela except the owner belong to the military sector.

3.6. Rio de Janeiro 646 (2436) (46 x 30 cm)

Two main people:
z3b sḥḏ zḫ3ww n nwt rsjt P3-ntj-nj (Franke, Doss. 231)
ḫtmtj-bjtj jmj-r3 pr wr Jmnw-m-ḥ3t Z3-Stjt (Franke, Doss. 85; also mentioned on Leiden 34)

Other people:
jmj-r3 pr n jmj-r3 ḫtmt Wr-n(.j)-Ptḥ (he also appears on Louvre C 39)
zḫ3w ʿn njswt n zm3jjt Jmnjj
dbḥn Ṯ3-n-mwt.f (?)

3.7. St. Petersburg Hermitage 1084 (Doss. 682); cf. *Snb-sw-m-ʿ(.j)*

3.8. Stockholm NME 31

stela of the *wʿb n Sbk nb Swmnw Wr-n.j-nṯr.j* (Doss. 211)

3.9. Wadi el-Hudi no. 23 (116 x 56 cm)

Main person (mentioned first in the text): *jdnw n jmj-r3 pr wr Jw-nfr*

šmsw n ʿrjjt Ḏdw-ṯnj
ḥrj n tm Bbj
ṯ3w ʿn zḫ3w ḥr ḫtm n wʿrt tp rsj Sbk-ḥtp
rḫ-njswt Snbw

jmj-rꜣ wꜥrt n Gbtj Bbj

3.10. Wadi el-Hudi no. 25 (28.5 x 17 cm)
dated to the 6th year of Sobekhotep IV
Main person: *ḫtmtj-bjtj [jmj-rꜣ pr wr] Nb-[ꜥ]nḫ* (Franke, Doss. 294)
zẖꜣw wr n ṯꜣtj Bbj

3.11. Vienna ÄS 144 (47.8 x 27.5 cm) The stela depicts the local elite around the stela owner, who was mayor at an unknown place. It is not certain that the stela belongs to the *Snbj* group, since the name and the titles of the main person are common.
Main person: *ḥꜣtj-ꜥ, jmj-rꜣ ḥwt-nṯr Zr* (Franke, Doss. 684, also mentioned on Leiden 34)
ꜣtjjt Jr-hb.s
jmj-rꜣ pr Jnpw.f
jmj-rꜣ ḫtmtjw Snb
jmj-rꜣ dpwt Ḫnms
zꜣw-ḥnkt Pjj
wḥmw Nb-j
wdpw Nrkkt
wdpw Zj-nj-Wsrt
mnꜥt ꜥfꜣ
mtj n zꜣ Snb.tjfj (Doss. 670 - common name and title)
ḥrj-pr Mꜣjj
ḥrj-pr Zꜣ-tp-jḥw
zẖꜣw ḥr ḫtmt Nḥjj
sftw Šd-wj-ḥr

List of stelae and other monuments which may be related to the above listed stelae. The monuments are mentioned first, followed by the person through whom the connection is possible and references to the relevant monuments (for further examples see Franke's dossiers).

Berlin 7286	(*jrj-ꜥt n wršw wnwtj Ḥtpj* also on Louvre C 45; Berlin 7286 is part of ANOC 18 - Cairo CG 20089, 20708)
Bologna KS 1929	(*ḥrj tm Bbj* - also on Leiden 33)
Cairo CG 20030	(*wdpw Wr-nb* also on Cairo CG 20266; Franke, Doss. 213)
Cairo CG 20039 and CG 20309	(*ṯsw n zẖꜣww qdwt Sḥtp-jb*, through Leiden 35)
Cairo CG 20266	(*jrj-ꜥt zꜣw jwf Wr-nb*, also on Cairo CG 20023; Franke, Doss. 212)
Copenhagen National Museum Ad10	(*jmj-rꜣ pr Nḥjj*, also on Heqaib no. 47. The name and title are common)
London BM 254	(*zꜣb sḥḏ zẖꜣww n nwt rsjt Pꜣ-ntj-nj,* also on Rio de Janeiro 646 (2436))
Louvre C 43	(*zꜣb sḥḏ zẖꜣww n nwt rsjt Pꜣ-ntj-nj* also on Rio de Janeiro 646 (2436))
Louvre C 45	(*wdpw n ꜥt t’ ꜥnḫw*, also on Cairo CG 20104)
Magdeburg	(*zẖꜣw n ḫnrt wr Jjj-jb, jmj-rꜣ pr ḥsb.... Jtjj* also on Tübingen 462; compare Franke, Doss. 20, 163, 711, 757)
New York, Brooklyn Museum acc.no. 08.480.176	(*ṯꜣw n ꜥt ḥnqt Rdj*; also on Copenhagen National Museum Ad 10; Franke, Doss. 351)
Tübingen 462	(*jmj-rꜣ pr Nḥjj*, also on Heqaib no. 47. The name and title are common).

Chapter 6
The *treasurers* after Sobekhotep IV

There are no monuments of *treasurers* datable to the time after Sobekhotep IV. In Vienna there is a stela of a *treasurer* named *Snb* (Vienna ÄS 145). From the style it is very likely that it belongs to the time of Neferhotep I and Sobekhotep IV. Though it seems that there is no space for another *treasurer* in this period he might date between *Snb-sw-m-*^{c}*(.j)* and *Snbj* or shortly after *Snbj*. Only this stela is known from him. He might therefore have been in office for a very short time. His mother might be a woman called *Rn-snb*, shown sitting in front of him on the stela. A *scribe of the treasury* called *Snb* is known from some other monuments (Franke, Doss. 611). The identification of these two people as one is not secure, as both names (*Snb* and *Rn-snb*) are very common.

Another *treasurer* who might date after Sobekhotep IV is *Jmnw-ḥtp*. He is mainly known from his burial in Dahshur (de Morgan 1903: 70, fig, 113; Franke, Doss. 87A) and from seals (Martin 1971: nos. 189-192; for the dating see Grajetzki 1995). From the writing of the title *ḫtmtj-bjtj* with the red crown, typical for the later part of the 13th Dynasty, the following *treasurers*, attested on seals, can be assigned to this period:

Jmnw-ḥtp (Martin 1971: nos.189-192)

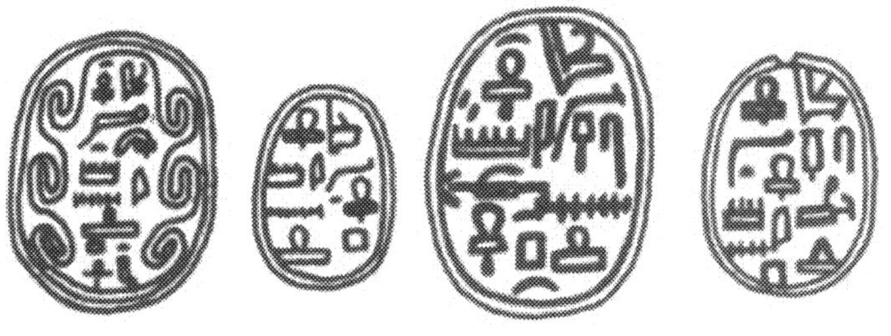

Jbt (Martin 1971: nos.109-111)

Jzj (Martin 1971: no. 274)

Wjn^{c} (Martin 1971: no. 256)

Nb-r-zḥwj (Martin 1971: nos. 663-670)

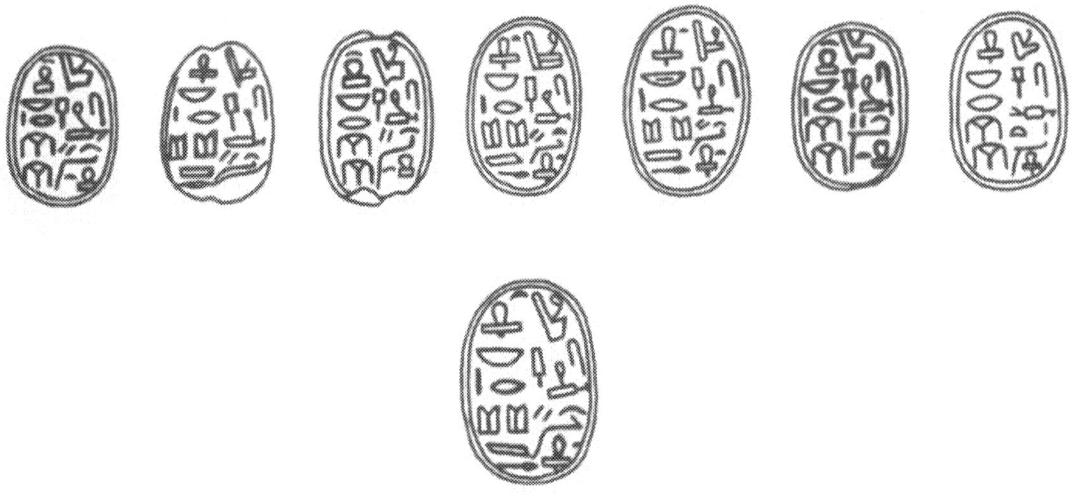

Nb-swmnw (Martin 1971: no. 682)

Rdj-n-Ptḥ (Martin 1971: nos. 898-902)

For a certain *...nḥw* (Martin 1971: no. 1785) the space where *ḫtmtj-bjtj* would have been written is lost. A closer look at all seals belonging to *treasurers* should be made to support the view that the writing of *ḫtmtj-bjtj* with the red crown is later than the writing with the bee. There are only five *treasurers* who are known from seals and from other monuments. Of these five *treasurers*, only two are datable through a king's name or links with other datable people. These are the *treasurers Snb-sw-m-ʿ(.j)* and *Snbj*. All their seals write *ḫtmtj-bjtj* with the bee. There is only one exception (Martin 1971: no. 1514) belonging to *Snb-sw-m-ʿ(.j)*. *Ḫrfw* and *Snb.f* have already been mentioned (chapter 3); from the style of their monuments (a stela and a weight) they might belong to the early 13th Dynasty. *Jmnw-ḥtp* might date shortly after Sobekhotep IV or even later. His seals show exclusively the writing with the red crown. He is not datable from his other monuments. However, the bad cutting of his seals also seems to point to a relatively late date.

It therefore seems to be the case that after Neferhotep I and Sobekhotep IV no stelae of a *treasurer* was set up in Abydos; at least there is no monument securely datable to this period. No stela or statue of a *treasurer* datable to this time is known from elsewhere. Examining the evidence for other officials the same observation holds good. There are only a few monuments of court officials datable after Sobekhotep IV. Only the stela of queen *Nbw-ḫʿj.s* might come from Abydos (Spalinger 1980). All other stelae mentioning high officials with ranking titles are either from Thebes (Bourriau 1988: 57-59, no. 45) or Elephantine. The custom of setting up a monument in Abydos is still well-attested in the 17th Dynasty. However, the general impression is that the scale of activity does not match that attested for the first part of the 13th Dynasty. The *treasurer* was an official working in the economic part of the palace. The kings at the end of 13th Dynasty seem to have been quite poor. It therefore does not seem very surprising that officials administering the poverty of a weak king were not themselves so important any more. The tomb of the *treasurer Jmnw-ḥtp* should be mentioned again. The tomb was badly looted, but the elaborate texts on the coffin and the position next to the tomb of a queen give the impression that the burial was of a quite high standard for its time.

A problem arises concerning some *treasurers* with foreign names also attested exclusively on seals. From the *treasurer Ḫ3r* more than 100 seals are known (Ryholt 1997: 60, n. 172). It is generally assumed that he was more or less contemporary with king Maaibre Sheshi (Ryholt 1997: 60; list of seals of the king: 366-376, File 14/5), who is also only known from scarabs. The date and position of king Maaibre Sheshi is far from certain. Ryholt recently dated him to the middle of the 14th Dynasty, and proposed that he was more or less contemporary with the middle 13th Dynasty (Ryholt 1997: 299). However his dating has not been widely accepted (Ben-Tor 1999). It would be best to say that there are no securely dated sources for the king and his *treasurer*, but it is highly likely that they were in someway connected with the high number of Palestinian Bronze Age people who lived in the Delta in the late 13th Dynasty and in the Second Intermediate Period. The *treasurer* is one of the few offices which can be placed with some certainty under the kings of the period. Therefore the impression is that this office was very important at that time. Since there are hardly any other offices recorded, there seems not to have been a very highly developed administration under the Asiatic kings. Maybe "*treasurer*" is just a translation of an Asiatic title which did not have much in common with the Middle Kingdom *treasurer*. Other *treasurers* attested on seals and dating to the Second Intermediate Period are: *Prj-m-ḥzt* (Martin 1971: nos. 477-506), *Rdj-ḥ3* (Martin 1971: nos. 904-912), *S3dj* (Martin 1971: no.1672). Only one *treasurer* can be placed with certainty in the 14th Dynasty. He is *Rn-snb*, who is known from a stela on which he is shown together with king Mer-djefa-Re (Yoyotte 1989). For the end of the Hyksos rule, two *treasurers* are recorded close to the king. *Jḥwjr* (the reading of the name is uncertain) is mentioned on a sphinx together with king Apophis (Goedicke 1977). A *treasurer* called *ꜥpr-bꜥ3rn* (Aper-baal) is known from two monuments. On an offering stand in Berlin (22487, only *ꜥpr*... survives from the name) he is mentioned together with king Apophis (Krauss 1993: 28, fig. 2), and he appears on a door lintel found at Tell Heboua (el-Maksoud 1998: 271-272, pl. I. with the full name *ꜥpr-bꜥ3rn*).

For the Egyptian 17th Dynasty before Kamose, no *treasurers* are recorded. The same is true of other officials connected with the *treasurers*. Hardly any *jmj-r3 st* or *jrj-ꜥt* is datable to the 17th Dynasty. This might have its reason in lack of sources, but it seems more likely that the administration under the *treasurer* simply became unimportant or even disappeared totally. The next Egyptian *treasurer* who is datable is *Nšj*, who appears on the Kamose stela (Helck 1975: 97, no. 119) very close to the 18th Dynasty.

Sequence of the *treasurers* from the 11th to the 17th Dynasty

11th Dynasty

Ṯtj	(Antef II)
Bbj	(Mentuhotep II - pre unification)
Ḫtjj	(Mentuhotep II)
Mkt-Rꜥw	(Mentuhotep II - Amenemhat I?)
Jnj-jtj.f	(late 11th - early 12th Dynasty)
Jpj	(late 11th - early 12th Dynasty)

12th Dynasty

Sbk-ḥtp	(Senusret I, 22nd year)
Mnṯw-ḥtp	(Senusret I)
Mrjj-k3w	(Amenemhat II)
Rḥw-r-ḏr.sn	(Amenemhat II)
Z3-3st	(Amenemhat II)

Sbk-m-ḥ3t	(Senusret III)
Sn-ᶜnẖ	(Senusret III, 8th year)
Zj-nj-Wsrt	(?Senusret III, 10th year)
Jjj-ḫr-nfrt	(Senusret III 19th year - Amenemhat III)

Late 12th or early 13th Dynasty

Jmnjj
Jmnjj
Jmnjj-snb
Ḥrw
Ḥrfw
Ḫpr-k3
Ḫntj-ḫtj)-m-z3.fSnb
Snb.f

First part of 13th Dynasty, only known from seals:

(ᶜḏ)-Zḥwj
Wpw-m-ḥ3b

Mid 13th Dynasty

Snb-sw-m-ᶜ(.j)	(before Neferhotep I)
Snbj	(Neferhotep I - Sobekhotep IV)
Snb	

Late 13th Dynasty

Jmnw-ḥtp
Jbt
Jzj
Wjnᶜ
Nb-r-zḥwj
Nb-swmnw
Rdj-n-Ptḥ

Second Intermediate Period, either 14th Dynasty or early 15th Dynasty

Prj-m-ḥzt	
Rn-snb	(Mer-djefa-Re)
Rdj-ḥ3	
Ḥ3r	
S3dj	

Hyksos (15th and 16th Dynasty)

ᶜpr-bᶜ3rn	(Apophis)
Jḥwjr	(Apophis)

17th Dynasty

Nšj	(Kamose)

It is highly likely that many *treasurers* are still missing from the list. No *treasurer* is known from the second half of the reign of Amenemhat I and the first half of the reign of Senusret I. No *treasurer* can be placed under Senusret II (through *Z3-3st* or *Sbk-m-ḥ3t* might have been *treasurer* under this king). The sequence of the *treasurers* from the time of Amenemhat III to the mid 13th Dynasty is totally unknown. The period covers about 80 to 90 years. There are about ten *treasurers* who can be placed for various reasons in this time. This would mean an average time in office of about 10 years for each of them. This might be possible during the 12th Dynasty, but seems unlikely for the unstable 13th Dynasty. In the mid 13th Dynasty only *Snb-sw-m-*^{c}*(.j)* and *Snbj* are accurately datable. The high number of monuments from *Snb-sw-m-*^{c}*(.j)* in particular makes it possible that he stayed in office a long time. However, there might be other reasons for the survival of his monuments and there might be other *treasurers*, like *Snb* who were in office under these kings. All the *treasurers* from the end of the 13th Dynasty are known so far only from seals and one burial; their sequence is not known.

Chapter 7
Royal activity in the mid 13th Dynasty in Abydos

In the course of examining the sources for *treasurers* in Abydos it becomes clear that they are well-attested at times when there is also evidence for increased royal building activity or at least for royal presence of some kind in this area. Several types of buildings by Middle Kingdom kings are attested in different areas of Abydos. The most important is the Osiris temple in the town. Many kings of the Old Kingdom built at this temple. In the Old Kingdom it was dedicated to Khenty-Imentiyw, who was identified with Osiris at least by the First Intermediate Period (Kemp 1975). The temple was excavated in 1902 -1903 and shortly afterwards published by Petrie (Petrie 1903, compare Kemp 1968). The whole area was already badly destroyed when Petrie arrived. The history of the temple is therefore very hard to follow. In the Middle Kingdom it seems to have been rebuilt or renewed first under Mentuhotep II (Petrie 1903: 14-16, pls. XXIV, LIV) and then again under Mentuhotep III Sankhkare (Petrie 1903: 16, pls. XXIII.5; XXV, LV; compare Kemp 1968: 140-141). Several blocks with the names of these two kings have been found. There are few sources for private activities in Abydos for this time. A remarkable exception might be a stela found in Abydos mentioning a *treasurer* with the name *Ḫtjj* (Peet/Loat 1913: pl. XXIX; Stewart 1979: no. 91, pl. 21 - Petrie Museum London UC 14430), who might be identical with the well-known *treasurer* from Thebes (Grajetzki 2000: 44-45, no. II.1). However there are no further titles - such as ranking titles - recorded on the stela so that the identification of the person mentioned on the stela from Abydos with the well-known *treasurer* cannot be proven. If the stela really belongs to the royal *treasurer* it could have been set up on the occasion of a visit by this official to Abydos. A possible reason for the visit would be building activity on behalf of the king.

Amenemhat I is so far only known in Abydos from a red granite offering table (Mariette 1880: 511, no. 1338). There are also not many private stelae found there datable to his reign (Simpson 1974: 26). From his successor more evidence from the temple has survived. Senusret I rebuilt the temple of Osiris (Petrie 1903: 16-17, pls. XXIII. 6-7, XXVI, LVI). It seems that the temple was very much enlarged and statues of the king were set up in it. It is highly likely that later kings of the 12th Dynasty also built at this temple, but the construction work of Senusret I was so important that it is even mentioned in a text of the 13th Dynasty as built by Senusret I (on stela Louvre C11). It is therefore no accident that under Senusret I the *treasurer Mnṯw-ḥtp* is so well-attested in Abydos (Simpson 1991: 332-335). He must have created an impressive chapel for himself in which the huge stela that was inscribed on both sides (CG 20539) and a false door (Boston MFA 1980.173; Freed 1996: 323-324) have survived. The next *treasurer* known from Abydos is *Rḥw-r-ḏr.sn* who also set up a stela (New York MMA 12.182.1; Freed 1996: 328-29), though this is quite modest in scale in comparison to the one from *Mnṯw-ḥtp*. *Rḥw-r-ḏr.sn* held office under Amenemhat II, for whom there is not much direct evidence in Abydos (cartouche - Simpson 1995: 36, 3 - fragment from a private stela?). However, there are two stelae now in London (BM 246 and 576) which mention a chapel or shrine (*ḥwt tpjjt*) of the king. The shrine might have been built in Abydos, though this is not certain (Fay 1996a: 41 with further literature). There are no monuments known at Abydos for the following *treasurers* until *Jjj-ḫr-nfrt*. The presence of *Jjj-ḫr-nfrt* there is well known. On his stela in Berlin he recorded the arrangements for the mysteries of Osiris. The stela bears the name of king Senusret III. From the temple of Osiris a statue of Senusret III is known (Petrie 1903: pl. XXVIII). The activity of the king in Abydos south is more important. Here he built a temple and a deep cut tomb (Wegner 1995) in which he might have been buried. Next to his temple he founded a town, which flourished into the Second Intermediate Period (Wegner 1998; Wegner 2000).

For the following *treasurers* only a few monuments have survived from Abydos. A block or fragment of a stela mentioning *Jmnjj-snb* was found at this site (Petrie 1925: pl. XXVIII) as well as the stela fragment of *Jmnjj*. (Petrie 1902: pl. LX.3, the position as *treasurer* is uncertain). The stela of *Snb.f* (Bosticco 1959: nos. 30a,b) might also come from here. Equally few monuments are known from kings of the late 12th Dynasty or early 13th Dynasty. From Amenemhat III there a lintel is known (Simpson 1995: 9-11, pl. 5). The famous 'Abydos princess' might also date on stylistic grounds to the reign of this king (Fay 1996b: 133-134). King Wegaf was probably responsible for a set of four stelae in the necropolis of Abydos of which one has survived and is now in the Cairo Museum (Leahy 1989: 48). The stela concerned arrangements of a holy district in the cemetery of Abydos: *two stelae are to be set up in its south and two in its north, carved with the great name of My Majesty.... as for anyone who shall be found within these stelae, except for a priest about his duties, he shall be burnt* (after Leahy 1989: 43; further literature - Ryholt 1997: 345, file 13/27, 11 and 12). The stela was later usurped by king Neferhotep I.

From king Sobekhotep (I) Kha-ankh-re some blocks with relief and an altar are attested. These are now in the Louvre and in Leiden (Bresciani 1979: 14 and passim). In the Osiris temple of Abydos Petrie found another relief fragment with the destroyed name of a king which might belong to about the same time (Petrie 1903: pl. XXIII.3; compare for another king of the 13th (?) Dynasty; Simpson 1995: 48, C 21). Finally, the Osiris bed found in Abydos should be mentioned. Leahy (1977: 433-434) proposed dating it under king Khendjer. This exact dating might not be correct (compare most recently; Ryholt 1997: 217 and Fay 1988: 70. n. 28). However, the work belongs to the 13th Dynasty.

The next well-attested *treasurer* in Abydos is *Snb-sw-m-^{c}(.j)*. While it is not really certain under which king *Snb-sw-m-^{c}(.j)* is to be dated, it can be shown that in the mid 13th Dynasty at least, beginning with Khendjer, there was again a higher level of interest in Abydos. On stela Louvre C11, datable via stela Louvre C12 (together ANOC 58) under king Khendjer, a narrative autobiographical passage relates the renovation of the temple built by Senusret I. The stela reports that the order for the renovation and cleaning (*sw^{c}b*) of the temple was given by the *vizier ^{c}nẖw*: *Behold, you are to clean this Temple in Abydos. Workmen will be given to you to execute it together with the priests of the temple of the nome, and the production place of the divine offering. Then I cleaned the outside and the inside in its walls. The scribe completed an image in pigment as renewing what Kheper-ka-re* (Senusret I) *had made.*

However, the most important source for royal activities in the 13th Dynasty is the great stela which king Neferhotep I set up in his second year. The king reports that he went to address his courtiers (*smrw*) and told them: *My heart wanted to see the scripts of old time of Atum, the great inventory was opened for me, so that I might know the god in his form and the ennead in its shape... that I might know the god in his form, that I might create it as in his oldest shape.* The following passage is especially important: *His majesty had summoned to him the rẖ-njswt who was next to his majesty. His majesty said to him: Start and sail south with a crew of workmen. They should not sleep at night or day till they reach Abydos.* (Helck 1975: 21-29 [32]; further literature is listed in Ryholt 1997: 245, file 13/27.12). The ensuing lines describe the making of the image of Osiris in the house of gold (*ḥwt-nbw*).

Another stela was usurped by Neferhotep I and mentioned a fourth year; it has already been described above. However apart from these stelae only a stone fragment with the name of Neferhotep I survives from Abydos (Petrie 1902: pl. LIX-bottom right). From his successor Sobekhotep IV fragments of doorjambs have been found at Abydos (Petrie 1903: pl. XXVIII). The findspot of the jambs shows that they might have been built as an entrance or doorway into the temple building of Senusret I, which was still standing then (Petrie 1903: 17, another relief of Sobekhotep IV from Abydos: Petrie 1902: pl. LIX) Little is known about the temple at this time. The few surviving monuments give the impression that it was filled with many stelae and statues from private individuals. In this respect the temple would have been very similar to the sanctuary of Heqaib on Elephantine. Finally, it should be mentioned that at Abydos south, near the large tomb of Senusret III some mastabas of the 13th Dynasty were found. A seal impression of a *vizier Jjj-mrw* was found there (Martin 1971: no. 49). Although there are several *viziers* with that name it is highly likely that the seal belongs to the *vizier* who served under Sobekhotep IV, because he seems to be the most important *vizier* of that name (Grajetzki 2000: 26-27, no. I.29). Although it is hard to determine what was really going on in Abydos south, the mastabas there and the seal impression might reflect some relatively large scale building activity in that area. *Snbj* is the last *treasurer* who is attested in Abydos. It is not possible to say if his activity is to be connected with Neferhotep I or Sobekhotep IV.

In the 12th Dynasty there is clearly a connection between the presence of the *treasurer* and royal activity in Abydos. Both *treasurers* who are well-attested in Abydos (*Mnṯw-ḥtp* ; *Jjj-ḫr-nfrt*) worked under kings who are also known for large scale building activity. As for the two *treasurers* of the 13th Dynasty who are again well documented in Abydos, it is more difficult to find out which king they served. The most important source is certainly the great stela of Neferhotep I, but it seems impossible to say whether *Snb-sw-m-^{c}(.j)* or *Snbj* are to be connected directly with the event described on the stela.

Chapter 8
People mentioned more than once on the stelae and monuments around the *treasurer*

Ꜣ3w-m-nwt, wdpw

He appears on stela Pittsburgh Acc.2983-6701 and on Roanne 163 in the second register. On stela Dublin UC 1360 he is shown in front of the main person, performing the king's offering. The two latter stelae belong to the *jmj-rꜣ st n jmj-rꜣ ḫtmt Rnpjj.f. Jꜣw-m-nwt* might therefore belong to the administration of *Rnpjj.f.*

Jꜣw-m-nwt is the main person on Chicago, Field Museum of Natural History no. 31647. The stela consists of two registers. In the first register stand *Jꜣw-m-nwt*, the *zj n dpwt-ꜥꜣt Snb-r-ꜣw* and a further person, whose name is lost. On the right stands the *wdpw n ꜥt jwf Jtjj*. In the second register are four women. *Jꜣw-m-nwt* is the only person in the stelae around the two *treasurers* with the low title *wdpw*, who is known from a monument of his own. However, a similar case might be the *wdpw n ꜥt jwf Mꜣꜥ-ḫrw* and the *zꜣw-ḫnkt Tjtj-ꜥnḫ*. Both men are known from stela Cairo CG 20556, where they are standing offering in front of the *jmj-rꜣ ꜥḫnwtj n kꜣp Tjtj*. On stela Cairo CG 20666 they appear as main people, maybe together with their wives. While the stela of the *jmj-rꜣ ꜥḫnwtj n kꜣp Tjtj* is a well made monument, the stela of the two less elevated men is of quite poor quality.

Jmnw-m-ḥꜣt Zꜣ-Stjt

Jmnw-m-ḥꜣt Zꜣ-Stjt is recorded on two stelae (Leiden 34, Rio de Janeiro 646 (2436)) as *high steward* and on two other stelae (Durham 1941, Moscow 5350) as mayor of Shedit (*ḥꜣtj-ꜥ jmj-rꜣ ḥmw-nṯr n Šdjt*). There is general agreement that they are the same person (Hodjash/Berlev 1982: 80; Franke, Doss. 85; Vernus 1986: 9, no. 27). *Jmnw-m-ḥꜣt Zꜣ-Stjt* was therefore a mayor who was appointed to the court with the position of *high steward*. On stela Leiden 34 he is shown sitting together with two other *high stewards*, and all have the ranking title *ḫtmtj-bjtj*. One might argue that they were responsible for products or estates in different regions. The appointment of a mayor as *high steward* recalls the career of the son of a nomarch from Beni Hasan, elevated to the court under Senusret III (Franke 1991).

ꜥnk.f

The *jmj-rꜣ ḫtmtjw jmj-jz ꜥnk.f* is the main person on Cairo CG 20023. A *high steward* with the same name and with the further title *jmj-jz* is attested on several seals (Martin 1971: nos. 345-347). They seem to be the same person.

Wr-n(.j)-Ptḥ

A person with this name and the title *jmj-rꜣ pr* is mentioned on the stela Cairo CG 20225. The stela belongs to *Snbj* as *rḫ-njswt*. On the stela Rio de Janeiro 646 (2436) a person with the same name appears with the title *jmj-rꜣ pr n jmj-rꜣ ḫtmt*. On this stela the *ḫtmtj-bjtj, jmj-rꜣ pr wr Jmnw-m-ḥꜣt Zꜣ-Stjt*, appears who is attested in the administration of the *treasurer Snbj* (on stela Leiden 34). An identification of both men with the name *Wr-n(.j)-Ptḥ* seems possible. *Wr-n(.j)-Ptḥ* would therefore have been a simple *jmj-rꜣ pr* in the private (?) household of an official at the beginning of his career. *Wr-n(.j)-Ptḥ* would have changed his title when his master was appointed to the position of *treasurer*.

Nb-jrwt (Doss. 287)

Nb-jrwt is recorded on Cairo CG 20718 as *jrj-ꜥt wdpw*. On stela Cambridge Fitzwilliam Museum E 1.1840 he is *wdpw jrj-jꜥḥ*, and finally on stela Cairo CG 20023 *jmj-rꜣ st*. On stela Turin inv. Cat. 1620 his title seems to have been deliberately destroyed. Stela Cairo CG 20023 is datable under Sobekhotep II. The career of *Nb-jrwt* therefore occurred mostly before that king.

Nb-ꜥnḫ (Spalinger 1980; Franke, Doss. 294; Grajetzki 2000: 93, III. 24; Franke 2001: 20)

Nb-ꜥnḫ is well-attested as *high steward* under Sobekhotep IV. He is mentioned together with the *treasurer Snbj* in the rock inscription de Morgan 1894: 87, no. 44. At this time he had the title *rḫ-njswt. Nb-ꜥnḫ* was one of several *rḫw-njswt* working in the administration of *Snbj. Nb-ꜥnḫ* was mainly on commission in the area of Aswan, while the other *rḫw-njswt* are mostly attested on stelae from Abydos. *Nb-ꜥnḫ* was later promoted to the office of *high steward*. His monuments as *high steward* are datable under Sobekhotep IV (rock inscription Wadi el-Hudi no. 25; Wadi Hammamat no. G 87) or even later (stela Louvre C 13).

N-mḥt-jb (Franke, Doss. 328)
The *wdpw n ꜥt tꜣ N-mḥt-jb* appears as *his beloved child* on stela Vienna ÄS 140 of *Snbj*. He is shown on stela Berlin 7311 in front of the *rẖ-njswt Rḥw-ꜥnẖ* offering two jars; from this context it seems clear that he belongs to the administration under *Rḥw-ꜥnẖ*, which might therefore also be true for stela Vienna ÄS 140. However, he might have been a real son of *Rḥw-ꜥnẖ*, especially given that he always appears in the context of the family of *Rḥw-ꜥnẖ*.

Rnpjj.f
(Franke 1994: 65, n. 18; Quirke 2000: 228-229)
The *jmj-rꜣ st Rnpjj.f* is mentioned twice together with *Snb-sw-m-ꜥ(.j)*: on Stela Pittsburgh Acc. 2983-6701 and on London BM 252. On Dublin UC 1360 he is the main person and on another stela (London BM 240) he and his wife (here *Jḥj*, instead of *Jtj* as on the other stelae) are the only people mentioned.

Rn-snb (Franke, Doss. 362)
A *zẖꜣw n ẖntj Rn-snb* appears on Cairo CG 20023 and on Cambridge Fitzwilliam Museum E 1.1840.

Rḥw-ꜥnẖ (Franke, Doss. 389)
Rḥw-ꜥnẖ is known from several stelae (Berlin 7311, Cairo CG 20104, CG 20147, Vienna ÄS 140) as *rẖ-njswt*. Two of these stelae belong to the *treasurer Snbj* (Cairo CG 20614, Vienna ÄS 140). The mining inscription Wadi el-Hudi no. 24 is dated to the 6th year of Sobekhotep IV and is the record of an expedition to procure amethyst. Four inscriptions are known from this expedition. In his analysis of these texts, Seyfried (1981: 121, 123-24, 129) questions if they are from one major expedition or from three small expeditions, because all the inscriptions mention different people. On Wadi el-Hudi no. 24 apart from the women of *Rḥw-ꜥnẖ* only the *jmj-rꜣ ꜥẖnwtj n kꜣp Snb* is recorded. This official also appears on several stelae there together with *Rḥw-ꜥnẖ*.

By examining the four stelae on which *Rḥw-ꜥnẖ* is mentioned, it might be possible to find out on what kind of occasion they were erected. Vienna ÄS 140 records the *treasurer Snbj* in the main position, but also includes the family of *Rḥw-ꜥnẖ*. Vienna ÄS 140 might therefore be some kind of family stela. Berlin 7311, which is very close in style to Vienna ÄS 140 and therefore very probably commissioned at the same time, might be some kind of personal stela. *Rḥw-ꜥnẖ*'s mother and wife are shown sitting in front of him, while servants/ his sons are making offerings. Stelae Cairo CG 20104 and CG 20147 record a number of lower-level palace officials and might have been set up by these officials to honor their master and at the same time provide an opportunity of appearing with their titles and names on at least one monument. It is therefore hardly surprising that not many of the people mentioned on the two stelae are found anywhere else.

It may be possible to follow the career of *Rḥw-ꜥnẖ* further. There are seals of an *overseer of the sealers Rḥw-ꜥnẖ* (Martin 1971: nos. 857-858) and there is a basalt statuette mentioned in the Černy notebooks of a *ẖtmtj-bjtj high steward Rḥw-ꜥnẖ*. While the *high steward* and the *overseer of the sealers* are most likely identical (see my previous discussion: Grajetzki 2000: 115), the identification with the *rẖ-njswt* follows only by analogy with the careers of *Nb-ꜥnẖ* and *Snbj-šrj*, both of whom occupied the position of *rẖ-njswt* before they became *high steward*.

"Lower part of a black basalt statuette", Černy notebook. 49 (PM VIII, 330 [801-413-600], Černy MSS. references and acknowledge Griffith Institute, Oxford)

Ḥrj-wꜣḥ
This official is attested on stela Roanne 163 as *jmj-rꜣ st n jmj-rꜣ ḫtmt*. On the stela Zagreb no. 8 he appears as *jrj-ꜥt*. Here he is called *ꜥꜣmw* - Asiatic. Both stelae are very similar in style, giving the strong impression that they were commissioned and produced at the same time. The two different titles can therefore probably be explained as two titles which *Ḥrj-wꜣḥ* held at the same time. There are secure attestations of officials carrying these titles together. However the possibility should also be kept in mind that *Ḥrj-wꜣḥ* was promoted while the stelae were being produced or that some time passed between the carving of the two stelae. On Zagreb no. 8 *Ḥrj-wꜣḥ* calls himself *the beloved son of the jrj-ꜥt n ꜥḥ Snfrw.*

Hr-nfr (Franke, Doss. 408)
Hr-nfr is attested on several monuments as *jmj-rꜣ ḫtmtjw*. On Leiden 14 he is mentioned together with *Snb-sw-m-ꜥ(.j)*. This is the only monument where he has no ranking titles. Cairo CG 20616 seems to be a stela set up by one of his servants (*ẖrd.f zꜣw-ḥnkt Hr-nfr*).

Ḫnms (Franke, Doss. 460)
On stela Cairo CG 20718 the *jrj-ꜥt wdpw Ḫnms* is mentioned together with *Snb-sw-m-ꜥ(.j)*. *Ḫnms* appears with the same title on stela Vienna ÄS 182 and on stela Cambridge Fitzwilliam Museum E.1.1840. On London BM 903 he appears as *jmj-rꜣ st*. On all other stelae (London BM 238; Marseilles no. 223; Turin inv. Cat. 1620; CG 20614) *Ḫnms* is recorded with the title *rḫ-njswt*. Especially from Marseilles no. 223, it is possible to reconstruct his family:

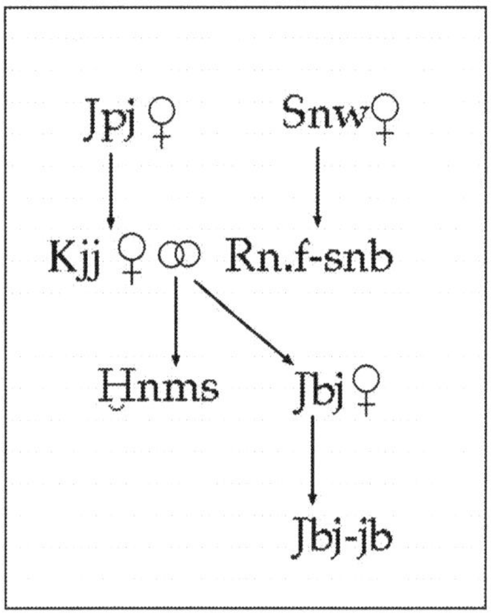

Zꜣ-Sbk
Zꜣ-Sbk appears on stela London BM 215 as *zḫꜣw qdt* and *ḥrj-ḥꜣb*. It therefore seems that he made the design for it including the drafts of the hieroglyphs. He appears again on stela Cairo CG 20479, which might be a stela of his own. Only a fragment remains naming *Zꜣ-Sbk* and a certain *Snfrw*.

Snb (Franke, Doss. 628)
The *jmj-rꜣ ꜥḫnwtj n kꜣp Snb* appears on several monuments (Wadi el-Hudi no. 24; Berlin 7311; Cairo CG 20614; Vienna ÄS 140) in connection with the *rḫ-njswt Rḥw-ꜥnḫ*. He is always recorded as second person after *Rḥw-ꜥnḫ*, but never as offering man. From stela Vienna ÄS 140 it is clear that the family of *Snb* was connected with the family of *Rḥw-ꜥnḫ*. The title *jmj-rꜣ ꜥḫnwtj n kꜣp* is closely related to food supply in the palace of the king.

Snbj-šrj
Snbj-šrj appears as *high steward* together with *Snb-sw-m-ꜥ(.j)* on stela St. Petersburg Hermitage 1084. He was therefore in office as *high steward* when *Snb-sw-m-ꜥ(.j)* was *treasurer*. A *high steward* called *Snbj*, born of *Jww*, is known from the statue base St. Petersburg Hermitage 5010 (pl. 4b). Stela Vienna ÄS 168 (pl. 4a) records a *rḫ-njswt Snbj-šrj* born of Iuui. The statue base in St. Petersburg dates - because of the writing of *ḫtmtj-bjtj* with the red crown - to the end of the 12th Dynasty or the 13th Dynasty. The identity of the three people depends on whether the *Snbj* from the statue base is to be identified with the two other people with the name *Snbj-šrj*. Since it is quite common in the Middle Kingdom to abbreviate a name (Vernus 1986: 113-115) there seems to be no problem with this identification.

Snfrw (Franke 1994: 66)
The *jrj-ꜥt n ꜥḥ Snfrw* has a statue of his own in the Heqaib Sanctuary (Habachi 1985: no. 69) on Elephantine. He is identified as born of the *nbt pr Rz*. He also appears on the stela Zagreb no. 8 which belongs to his son *Ḥrj-wꜣḥ*.

Snn (Franke, Doss. 682; Franke 1994: 66)
The *rḫ-njswt Snn* is mentioned on one monument together with *Snb-sw-m-ꜥ(.j)* (St. Petersburg Hermitage 1085) and on two monuments together with *Snbj* (Cairo CG 20614; Liverpool no. M13661). His time in office must have spanned the last years of *Snb-sw-m-ꜥ(.j)* and at least the first years of the *treasurer Snbj*. On the stela Liverpool no. M13661 he is clearly the most important person, appearing in the first place in the offering formula and standing on the left side. On the stela Cairo CG 20614 he is sitting in front of the *treasurer*, almost equal to him with an offering formula of his own. *Snn* also appears on Vienna ÄS 200; a rectangular stela with a cornice. *Snn* is the only person mentioned on it. He is sitting in front of an offering table. At the top of the stela two names are incised in hieratic. Only the outlines of the figures are incised, and the workmanship is rather poor. *Snn* is the owner of a statue found at the sanctuary of Heqaib at Elephantine (Habachi 1985: 89-90, no. 63). Little is known of his social background and his family. His mother is the *nbt pr Ttj*, and his father is called *Kmn.j* and bears the title *sns*: This title is not well-attested; little can be said about it's meaning (Ward 1982: 1316 - *hairdresser* ?; Fischer 1997: 73 - *mourner*). There is a *ḫtmtj-bjtj, jmj-rꜣ sḏtjw Snn* attested on a seal (Martin 1971: no. 1623); it seems possible that he is identical with the *rḫ-njswt*. A similar career is attested elsewhere (Berlev 1974a; Grajetzki 2000: 180, no. XI.6).

Sbk-ḥr-ḥꜣb (Franke, Doss. 570)
On several stelae a person called *Sbk-ḥr-ḥꜣb* appears with various titles. Only one of these records the filiation, and the identity is therefore not secure: Franke (Doss. 570) gives a question mark for the identification. However, in general there is no problem with bringing all the people with the name *Sbk-ḥr-ḥꜣb* together, in particular as it can be shown that *Sbk-ḥr-ḥꜣb* is very often connected with *Ḫnms*. Both officials seem to have followed the same career at about the same time.
Following attestations for *Sbk-ḥr-ḥꜣb* are to be found:

Vienna ÄS 182: *jrj-ꜥt wdpw* (without filiation) together with the *jrj-ꜥt wdpw Ḫnms*.
Cairo CG 20718: *jrj-ꜥt wdpw* (without filiation) together with the *jrj-ꜥt wdpw Ḫnms*.
Munich 36: *jrj-ꜥt wdpw* (without filiation)
Cambridge Fitzwilliam Museum E.1.1840: *wdpw jrj-jꜥḥ* (mother: *Npt-rjt*) together with the *jrj-ꜥt wdpw Ḫnms*.
London BM 428: *jrj-ꜥt n Kpnj* (without filiation)
Marseilles no. 223: *rḫ-njswt* (without filiation) together with the *rḫ-njswt Ḫnms*.
Leiden 34: *rḫ-njswt* (without filiation; the name is written *Sbk-ḥꜣb*)

Sbk-ḥtp (Franke, Doss. 583)
An *jrj-ꜥt wdpw Sbk-ḥtp* appears on Cairo CG 20718 and on Cambridge Fitzwilliam Museum E 1.1840. The identification as one person is - because of the common name and common title - far from certain.

Sbk-ḥtp (Franke, Doss. 591)
The *jmj-rꜣ ꜥḫnwtj ḫrp sk Sbk-ḥtp* is known from several different objects; many of them are his own monuments. On stela St. Petersburg Hermitage 1084 he appears together with *Snb-sw-m-ꜥ(.j)*. With the stela belongs the offering table Marseilles no. 252, where he is also mentioned. The stela London BM 238 (the main person on the stela is *rḫ-njswt Ḫnms*) is datable a little later. *Sbk-ḥtp* is mentioned on it next to his colleague *Snb.f* who bears the same title. All other monuments of *Sbk-ḥtp* are his own. The stela Cairo CG 20353 (21 x 18 cm; Abydos, nördliche Umwallung, Kom es Sultan) is not typical since it has only two short inscriptions, a prayer to Osiris and the name/title of *Sbk-ḥtp*. Instead of a scene there is a big ankh-sign in the middle of the stela. There are also two statue bases belonging to him (Cairo CG 1246, CG 1247), both from Abydos, and he is mentioned in a rock inscription (De Morgan 1894: 90, no. 84bis).

Kkw (Franke, Doss. 725)
A *zḫꜣw pr ꜥnḫ Kkw* appears on Cairo CG 20023 and on Cambridge Fitzwilliam Museum E 1.1840.

Tjtj,
(full list of monuments: Franke, Doss. 732; Grajetzki 2000: III.18)
Date: This person can be dated through stela Cambridge Fitzwilliam Museum E.1.1840 to about the same time as *Snb-sw-m-ᶜ(.j)*. The career of *Tjtj* is of special interest because it is possible to follow him from being a common *wdpw* to the middle ranking title *jmj-r3 ᶜẖnwtj n k3p* and then to the high-level position of an *overseer of sealers* and a *high steward*. In his career *Tjtj* covers all of the social levels proposed in this study on the basis of the mid 13th Dynasty stelae.

Chapter 9
Specific titles

rḫ-njswt
(Doxey 1998: 125)

The title *rḫ-njswt* is already well-attested as a ranking title in the Old Kingdom (Jones 2000: 327-328, no. 1206: Baud 1999: 107-112), mainly for people with a not very high position in the administration. In the First Intermediate Period there are not many people recorded with the title, but it become quite common again in the Middle Kingdom. In the Early Middle Kingdom there are two groups of people with the ranking title *rḫ-njswt*. On the one hand are numerous high officials with the highest ranking titles (*jrj-pꜥt, ḥꜣtj-ꜥ, ḫtmtj-bjtj, smr-wꜥtj*), who also bear the title *rḫ-njswt* (good datable examples are: Louvre C1, Louvre C2, Leiden 6). So far, no official with these highest titles and the title *rḫ-njswt* is attested later than Senusret III (last datable example: statue London BM 100, compare for the dating: Franke, Doss. 257). However under Amenemhat II *rḫ-njswt* had already fallen out of use in strings of ranking titles (Grajetzki 2000: 225-226). On the other hand there are officials who are exclusively recorded with a function title and the ranking title *rḫ-njswt*. These people seem to have had a position just under the highest officials with ranking titles. These officials are attested throughout the Middle Kingdom, though no longer so often in the Late Middle Kingdom (examples from the 13th Dynasty: Wadi el-Hudi no. 155; Cairo CG 20089, Berlin 7286; Boston MFA 72.766a&b; Leprohon 1985: 1-5). In the Late Middle Kingdom *rḫ-njswt* is also often recorded as the sole title of a person and it seems that it had become a function title for people directly connected with the royal court. There are two ways of interpreting the Late Middle Kingdom use of the title:

1. *Rḫ-njswt* was still used as a ranking title and could replace the function title before the name in some circumstances.
2. *Rḫ-njswt* was a function title in the Late Middle Kingdom. It was the main designation of the official who held it.

In support of the first idea one might draw on the evidence for people with the title *jmj-rꜣ st* (cf. discussion of the title for the people and further reference). There are three people in the 12th Dynasty recorded with the title *jmj-rꜣ st* and the ranking title *rḫ-njswt*. In the 13th Dynasty there is evidence for officials who are recorded on one monument as *jmj-rꜣ st* and on another as *rḫ-njswt*. At present it is not really possible to say if these monuments are more or less contemporary. Could an official of the 13th Dynasty bear the titles *jmj-rꜣ st* and *rḫ-njswt* at the same time (already Berlev 1978: 256, compare the discussion of *jrj-ꜥt wdpw*)? Are the stelae set up at a different time? Are these titles two steps of a career?

From the many stelae showing a *rḫ-njswt* in the main position it seems to be quite certain that people with this title occupied an important position at court which was just under the officials with ranking titles.
The following stelae of the groups already discussed show a *rḫ-njswt* in the main position (with the name of the title holder):

Berlin 7311	(*Rḥw-ꜥnḫ*)
Cairo CG 20104	(*Rḥw-ꜥnḫ*)
Cairo CG 20147	(*Rḥw-ꜥnḫ*)
Cairo CG 20225	(*Snbj*)
Cairo CG 20282	(*Snn*)
Liverpool no. M13661	(*Snn*)
London BM 238	(*Ḫnms*)
Louvre C39	(*Snbj*)
Marseilles no. 223	(*Ḫnms*)
Turin inv. Cat. 1620	(*Ḫnms*)
Wadi el-Hudi no. 24	(*Rḥw-ꜥnḫ*)

Titles which appear more than once on these stelae:
zꜣw-ḫnkt (x3), *wdpw* (x2), *zḫꜣw n ḫntj* (x2), *ḥrj-pr n pr-ꜥꜣ* (x2), *wdpw n ꜥt tꜣ* (x2), *ꜥnḫ n tt ḥqꜣ* (x2), *šmsw* (x2), *jmj-rꜣ ꜥḫnwtj n kꜣp* (x2).

This list calls for some comments. Most of the stelae seem to date under the *treasurer Snbj* or belong to him before he became *treasurer*. The appearance of some titles on these stelae might simply have something to do with the fact that a title holder is related via his family to the main person on the stela (cf. the *jmj-r3 ꜥḫnwtj n k3p Snb*). However, in general the dominant titles are again those connected with food production at the palace, in which the *rḫ-njswt* seems to be an important person. Indeed the holder of the title sometimes seems equal in position even to the *treasurer*, as can be seen from *Snn*, on the stela Liverpool no. M13661, who he is shown as more important than the *treasurer* himself.

The title *rḫ-njswt* appears in the great inscription of Neferhotep I from Abydos (compare p. 41). The king summons the *rḫ-njswt* who is beside him and send him on a mission to Abydos. The phrase *rḫ-njswt* might denote position, rather than one precise function. The *smrw* mentioned at the beginning of the text are presumably the highest courtiers with ranking titles (Grajetzki 2000: 224-225), while the title *rḫ-njswt* seems to be just one level under the highest courtiers. The expression *rḫ-njswt* in this text might be a designation for a class of officials. The stela creates the impression that the *smrw* are officials around and in very close contact with the king. In this context, in contrast to *smr*, the *rḫ-njswt* is an official who is travelling around the country on commission for the king. A further observation points in the same direction. Officials attested in expedition inscriptions in the late 12th Dynasty quite often bear the ranking title *rḫ-njswt*, whereas higher ranking titles are not often attested. High ranking titles are known from only a few expedition inscriptions of the 13th Dynasty (Wadi el Hudi, Sadek 1980: 52, no. 25), but one wonders if these high officials really went on the expedition; it seems more plausible that other people with the ranking title *rḫ-njswt* (Sadek 1985: 5-7, no. 155) or sole title *rḫ-njswt* (Sadek 1980: 51, no. 24) might have been the real leaders.

ḥrj-pr n pr-ꜥ3

This title is one of the most common on the stelae described here. The title *ḥrj-pr* is discussed by Berlev (1978: 129-161, list of *ḥrj-pr n pr-ꜥ3*: 133). He comes to the conclusion (op. cit.: 130-131) that the *ḥrj-pr* did not work in the *šnꜥw* (the place of food production in the palace), but in the private part of the house, looking after the valuables (linen, furniture etc.) of the house owner, while the *jmj-r3 pr* was concerned with the estates of an individual or institution. The *ḥrj-pr n pr-ꜥ3* therefore worked in the residential part of the palace.

ḫkrt-njswt

This title was discussed by Drenkhahn (1976) who does not try to date the occurrences of the title and who concentrates almost exclusively on the sources of the Old and New Kingdoms. She comes to the conclusion that the title refers to women belonging to the court but who do not have sexual contact with the king, an idea that was formerly an explanation for this title. Brack (1984, with older literature) comes to the conclusion for the New Kingdom that the title might refer to women who had intimate contact to the king. Ward (1986: 14) states that most of the attestations from the Middle Kingdom belong to the earliest Middle Kingdom. A closer look at the references given by Ward (1982: no. 1233; for no. 1234 - *ḫkrt-njswt wꜥtt* - most references belong to the Early Middle Kingdom; compare Franke 1990: 229) reveals that numerous examples for the title belong to the Late Middle Kingdom and the Second Intermediate Period (compare Vernus 1974: 110 and the table on 113), while the earlier references mostly belong to the First Intermediate Period. From the list, in which all known titleholders for the Late Middle Kingdom are collected, it can be seen that the title was not current in the 12th Dynasty.

The earliest attestation of the late Middle Kingdom dates under Senusret III - Amenemhat III, and belongs to a woman who seems to be the wife of a very high official whose name and titles are lost. The tomb of this man is about the same size as the nearby tomb of the *vizier Nb-jt* (Arnold 1996: 25; Grajetzki 2000: 17, I.11 compare n. 1), so it is extremely likely that he held a very high position, maybe even a *vizier*. The next datable woman with the title *ḫkrt-njswt* is found on stela Würzburg N.35 (Berlev 1974b), where a *ḫkrt-njswt* is sitting behind the *king's wife Jjj*. The stela belongs to the extensive family of the *vizier ꜥnḫw*. The *ḥmt njswt Jjj* is the wife of king Sobekhotep II known from pBoulaq 18, where she is also attested. Sadly, only the lower half of the Würzburg stela has survived. The upper half is broken away exactly at the point where a filiation should appear. In the lowest register two people are mentioned as *his brother* and *his daughter*. Although it is not possible to prove, it seems likely that the monument was a family stela. The queen and the *ḫkrt-njswt* would then be members of the same family. The next datable example is *N-qr-ḥrj-jb* on stela Liverpool no. M13635, where it is also possible to postulate a close connection to the royal court. Finally, there are two women with the title mentioned on stela Louvre C 13 belonging to queen *Nbw-ḫꜥj.s*. The stela might date shortly after Sobekhotep IV. All other datable attestations belong to the later 13th Dynasty (London BM 1348 - king Ibiau; the reading of the title is not certain; BM 1163 - king Sobekemsaf I; Moscow I Ia 5358 - king Sewahenre; Clère 1982: pl. VI - king Rahotep; New York MMA 35.7.55, Hayes 1947). All other monuments mentioning the title - in particular the stelae - seem to be rather late, judging from their style. Most of the title holders on these late monuments are no longer women directly connected with the royal court. Their husbands occupy positions just under the highest officials. The only exception might be *Ḫnsw*, the wife of an official who is attested as *rḫ-njswt* but also as *ḫtmtj-bjtj jmj-rꜣ sḫtjw*. The title *ẖkrt-njswt* appears on her coffin and canopic box. On the same objects her husband is only called *rḫ-njswt* (Grajetzki 2000: 180, no. XI.6). Titles such as *ꜣtw n ṯt ḥqꜣ* and *wr mḏw Šmꜥw* which are very common for the husbands of the *ẖkrt-njswt* (Vernus 1974: 113) seem to belong to the highest social level in the late 13th and 17th Dynasties. However, it should be stated that we do not know anything about the families of the officials with ranking titles in the latest Middle Kingdom. The title *ẖkrt-njswt* is also attested in the late 13th Dynasty in the provinces where it is sometimes found worn by the wife of a *mayor* or *overseer of priests* (Cairo CG 20530; New York MMA 35.7.55).

Taking all sources for the Late Middle Kingdom together, it seems that initially the title was given to women who were very closely linked to the royal court, maybe through some kind of family relationship. The evidence from the 11th Dynasty in Thebes points in the same direction: the title was given to several women who also had the title *king's wife* (Naville 1907: pl. VII, XX). After Sobekhotep IV the title became more popular and it seems that to some extent it replaced *nbt pr*. The titles *bꜣkt nt ḥqꜣ* and *ꜥnḫt nt tpt njswt* (Ward 1986: 61-65) became also important. *Nbt pr*, which had been so common in the late 12th and early 13th Dynasty, never totally disappeared.

List of titleholders from the Late Middle Kingdom
(Name of title holder; title of husband; reference):

Jꜥt-jb	*zꜣb*	Downes 1974: 73
Jw-snb	*ꜣtw n ṯt ḥqꜣ*	Chicago Field Museum of Natural History 31679
Jwḥt-jb	*wr mḏw Šmꜥw*	Cairo CG 20661
Jwḥt-jb	*zẖꜣw ḥwt-nṯr*	London BM 1163 (datable under Sobekemsaf I)
Jr...	*ꜣtw n ṯt ḥqꜣ*	Vienna ÄS 196
Jrj.s	*ꜣtw n ṯt ḥqꜣ*	Berlin 7287, Berlin 1913: 203
Jrj-tm-jb		*zẖꜣw ḥwt-nṯr* statue Paris Louvre AF 9916, Delange 1987: 222-223 (from Elephantine)
Jtj-ꜥnḫ	*zꜣb*	Peet 1914: 114, fig. 71, no. 11
Mwt-ꜥnḫ.tj	*ꜣtw n ṯt ḥqꜣ*	Moscow I.1.a.5608 (4157); Hodjash/Berlev 1982: no. 38
Nbw ...	*wr mḏw Šmꜥw*	Louvre C 190, she is *ẖkrt-njswt wꜥtj(t)*
Nbw-Jwnt	*rꜣ-Nḫn*	Cairo CG 20668
Nbw-Jwnt	*ꜣtw n ṯt ḥqꜣ*	Garstang 1901: pl. XIII
Nbw-jb	*rḫ-njswt*	Bolton 10.20/12, Donohue 1966: fig on p.19
Nbw-m-ḥꜣb (?)	*jmj-rꜣ šnṯ*: Cairo CG 20373=	Franke, Doss. 584
Nbw-m-ḥꜣb	*wr ḫrp ḥmww*	Cambridge Fitzwilliam Museum E.SS.37, Bourriau 1982: 51-55, pl. III.1
Nbw-ḥr-rdj	*ꜣtw n ṯt ḥqꜣ*	Cairo CG 28030 (wife of CG 28126; compare Franke, Doss. 412)
Nbw-ḫꜥj.s	*ḥm-nṯr n Ḥrw Nḫn*	Cairo CG 20530
Nbw-ḫꜥj.s	*zꜣb rꜣ-Nḫn*	Vernus 1986

Nbw-ḥꜥj.s	*jmj-rꜣ ṯbw*	Cairo CG 20322, also mentioning people with the titles *ꜣṯw n ṯt ḥqꜣ* and *zꜣb rꜣ-Nḫn.*
Nfr-ḥtp	*zꜣb*	Downes 1974: 74, fig. 38
Nfrt-wbn	*ꜣṯw n ṯt ḥqꜣ*	Cairo CG 20668/ Petrie 1902: pl. 59 = Franke, Doss. 576
Ḫpw	*jmj-rꜣ nbw*	Randall-MacIver/Mace 1902: pl. XXXIV.2
Ḫr (?)-m-ḥꜣb	*zꜣ-njswt tpj*	Cairo CG 20732
H̱nsw	*rḫ-njswt -> ḫtmtj-bjtj jmj-rꜣ sḫtjw*	Moscow I Ia 5358, Berlev 1974a: pl. XXVI (datable under king Sewahenre)
Sbk-nḫt	*sḥḏ ḥmw-nṯr tpj n Nḫn jmj-rꜣ ꜣḥwt*	New York MMA 35.7.55 from Hierakonpolis; Hayes 1947: 4 (late 13th Dynasty)
Snb.s-ꜥnḫ.s	*wr mḏw Šmꜥw*	Vienna ÄS 180
Snb.tjsj	*jmj-rꜣ pr ḥsb jt*	Tübingen 462 (*ḫkrt-njswt wꜥtjt* - about Sobekhotep IV)

Title holders whose husbands are not identified:

NN (name lost)	- Cambridge Fitzwilliam Museum E.67.1932; Bourriau 1988: no. 37 (wrongly described as king's sister);
Jꜥw-jb	- Cairo CG 20322, people with the titles *jmj-rꜣ ṯbw, ꜣṯw n ṯt ḥqꜣ* and *zꜣb rꜣ-Nḫn* are also mentioned.
Jꜥt-jb	- London UC 14214; Petrie 1909: pl. XXX. 6
Jw-snb	- Paris Louvre C 13; stela with the extended family of queen *Nbw-ḥꜥj.s*
Jwj ?	- Peet 1914: 115, fig. 73, no. 13, also mentioned: *jmj-rꜣ ḥzw, ꜣṯw n ṯt ḥqꜣ, rꜣ-Nḫn*
Jwrrj	- mother of the *zꜣ-njswt Bb*, Durham n. 1984, Bourriau 1988: no. 52
Jbr...,	- Cairo CG 20486, people with the titles *zꜣb rꜣ-Nḫn* and *wr mḏw Šmꜥw* are mentioned on the stela
Jnj-jtj.f	- Würzburg N. 35 (date: Sobekhotep II), a *king's wife* appears also on the stela, Berlev 1974b
Jrmḥj	- Martin 1971: no. 270
ꜥkw (two women with this name)	- Cairo CG 20058, the stela belongs to a *zꜣt-njswt*
Bn-ḥr-jnḏ-jb	- Cairo CG 20486, people with the titles *zꜣb rꜣ-Nḫn* and *wr mḏw Šmꜥw* are mentioned on the stela
Mw-nw-jb	- Martin 1971: no. 541
Nbw-m-tḫj, Nbw-ḥꜥj.s, Zꜣt-Jmnw,	three women with the title on the fragment of a large stela, one of the men has the title *ꜣṯw n ṯt ḥqꜣ*, Petrie 1902: 43, pl. 60
N-qr-ḥrj-jb	- Liverpool no. M13635, mother of a *zꜣt-njswt* (Neferhotep I - Sobekhotep IV)
Nbw	- Franke 1994: pl. 9 (end of 17th Dynasty, Franke 1994: 87)
Nbw-ꜥ.s-mw-jb (?)	- Cairo CG 20486, people with the titles *zꜣb rꜣ-Nḫn* and *wr mḏw Šmꜥw* are mentioned on the stela
Nbw-ḥr-mr.s (?)	- Cairo CG 20486, persons with the titles *zꜣb rꜣ-Nḫn* and *wr mḏw Šmꜥw* are mentioned on the stela
Nbw-ḥtp.tj (x2), *Jꜥw-jb*	- Cairo CG 20322, people with the titles *jmj-rꜣ ṯbw, ꜣṯw n ṯt ḥqꜣ* and *zꜣb rꜣ-Nḫn* are also mentioned.
Nfrw	- Paris Louvre C 13, family stela of queen *Nbw-ḥꜥj.s*
Nfrw	- statue Cairo CG 1039 (*ḫkrt-njswt wꜥtjt*)
Nfrt	- coffin New York MMA, Hayes 1953: 348 ("the royal ornament Nyet-nefret", compare Willems 1988: 33, T5NY)
Nfrt.sj-m-jb	- mother of a *king's son*, Downes 1974: 76, fig. 40
Nnj	- Martin 1971: no. 755
Nḫtj	- Paris Louvre AF 9919, Delange 1987: 226 (from Elephantine)

R-ḥtp-nbw	- Martin 1971: no. 809
Rn-snb	- London BM 1348, Bourriau 1988: 57-59, no. 45 (dated under king Ibiau, to read *ḥm-njswt* ?, compare Berlev 1972b: 12)
Ḥpt-rḥw	- Cairo CG 20373
Ḥrw...	- Petrie 1903: pl. XXX.5, other titles mentioned on the stela: *ꜣṯw n ṯt ḥqꜣ, zꜣb rꜣ-Nḫn*
Ḫnsw, Nfrt-wbn	(the latter is the mother of a *zꜣb rꜣ-Nḫn*) stela London Petrie Museum UC 14418, Stewart 1979: 27, no. 113, pl. 28.3
Zꜣt-wrwt	- wife of a high official whose name and title are lost, Arnold 1996: 24 (compare Grajetzki 2000: 17, n. I.11); dating: Senusret III - Amenemhat III
Sbk-ḥtp	- Athen no. 10, daughter of a *wr mḏw Šmꜥw*
Skt (mother of a *king's son*)	- Martin 1971: no. 1314
Kwms	- Clère 1982: pl. VI (datable under king Rahotep)

jmj-rꜣ ḫtmtjw

This title is discussed in Grajetzki 2000: 146-157. People with the title *jmj-rꜣ ḫtmtjw* appear on several stelae as main person and on some other stelae as one of two main figures.

Stelae of *jmjw-rꜣ ḫtmtjw*

1. Cairo CG 20023
2. Cairo CG 20087 (together with a *high steward*)
3. Cairo CG 20396
4. Cairo CG 20616
5. Cambridge Fitzwilliam Museum E 1.1840 (together with an *jrj-ꜥt wdpw*)
6. London BM 210 (together with an *jmj-rꜣ st*)
7. London BM 903
8. New York MMA 68.14

Even though there are quite a number of titles attested on more than one stela, it is very hard to judge to which part of the administration the people under the *jmj-rꜣ ḫtmtjw* belonged. The sources give the impression that a totally different kind of official appears on each stela. Stela no. 8 (New York MMA 68.14) is entirely military in character; no. 7 belongs to people working in the food production part of the palace, while on 1 and 2 numerous people appear who seem to belong to different areas of the palace. On 1 and 5 a title like *zẖꜣw n pr-ꜥnḫ*, appears (both attestations belong to the same person: *Kkw*) which is not very common in the Middle Kingdom (Ward 1982: no. 1380).

The titles which appear more than once are: *zẖꜣw n ḫntj* (nos. 1, 5, 7); *ṯꜣw n ḫft-ḥr* (nos. 1, 5); *jmj-rꜣ st* (nos. 1, 4); *šmsw* (nos. 7, 8); *zẖꜣw n pr-ꜥnḫ* (nos. 1, 5). However, the most common title is *zẖꜣw n ḫntj* which clearly belongs to the food production sector of the palace. The general impression is therefore that the *jmj-rꜣ ḫtmtjw* worked in different parts of the palace with a focus on food production.

Titles of the *šnꜥw*
(Berlev 1978: 235-327; Franke 1983b)
The following titles are very common on the monuments around the *treasurers*. They all belong to the administration of the *šnꜥw*, which was the food producing sector of the palace. It has been possible to show (chapters 2 and 3) that many of the following titles already appear under Senusret III in connection with the *treasurer*. Others are not yet attested with this office at the beginning of the Late Middle Kingdom but this may only reflect the uneven survival of sources. The titles themselves are already well-attested at this time (see *zẖꜣw n ḫntj*). A few of the following titles are only know from the 13th Dynasty (*jmj-rꜣ st n ꜥt* + additional expression). They might have been introduced at that time. One general and still unanswered question arises: are these titles really introduced under Senusret III or in the 13th Dynasty or are they only visible for the first time in the sources then? It seems impossible at the moment to decide this question, but it should be observed that only very little is known about the administration under the *treasurer* in the Early Middle Kingdom.

jmj-rꜣ ꜥḫnwtj n kꜣp

(Gauthier 1918: 195-197; Ward 1982: no. 91; Quirke 1990: 106-107)

Jw-snb	stela, Cairo CG 20693, Louvre C 45 (Sobekhotep IV)
Jṯnw	seal, Martin 1971: no. 299a
ᶜnḫj	seal, Martin 1971: no. 334
ᶜnḫ.tjfj	stela, Cairo CG 20614 (stela of *Snbj*)
Bmbw	stela, Louvre C 13 (*jmj-r3 ᶜẖnwtj wr n k3p*)
Ptḥ-wr	seal, Martin 1971: no. 520
Mnw-ḥtp	seal, Martin 1971: no. 554
Mmj	stela, Cairo CG 1263 (statue, Franke 1994: 65)
Mswt	seal, Martin 1971: nos. 621-624
Nḫjj	seal, Martin 1971: no. 764
Rn-snb (Jmj-ẖnt ?)	seal, Martin 1971: no. 816
Rn.f-m-jb	pBoulaq 18
Rḥw-r-3w	de Morgan 1894: 11, nos. 33; 84, nos. 9; 86, no. 34 (Franke, Doss. 390)
Rzw-nfr	seal, Martin 1971: no. 869
Ḥrj-Snfrw Rn.f-snb	stela, Turin inv. Cat. 1626
Snb	stelae, Berlin 7311, Cairo CG 20614, Vienna ÄS 140 seal, Martin 1971: no. 1480 (stelae of *Snbj*)
Snb.f	stela, Turin inv. Cat. 1627
Snb.f	stela, Cairo CG 20054
Snb.tjfj	Arnold 1990: 178, kh 8 - date: Khendjer
Kkj	pBoulaq 18
Tjtj	stelae, Cairo CG 20556; Vienna ÄS 143; seal, Martin 1971: no. 1719
Ṯmj	seal, Martin 1971: no. 1738

As far as it is possible to tell, all of the people with this title are datable to the 13th Dynasty. The only exception might be one seal (Martin 1971: no. 816) which belongs to the back type (backtype 3) from the late 12th Dynasty. From pBoulaq 18 it is known that there could be two people with this title at the royal court at one time. This is also clear from stela Cairo CG 20614, where two title holders are recorded together.

jmj-r3 st

The title *jmj-r3 st* is well-attested from the time of the Old Kingdom (Jones 2000: 239, no. 876) and is also very common in the Middle Kingdom (Ward 1982: no. 313). It is known from the royal court and is also well-attested at provincial courts (Beni Hasan: Newberry 1893: pls. XVII-XX, XXXV). In particular from the stelae around *Snb-sw-m-ᶜ(.j)* and *Snbj* it is obvious that the *jmj-r3 st* was partly in charge of the different chambers of food production. He might have been the direct head of this part of administration with the *wdpw* under him. Other sources reveal a strong link with the title *jrj-ᶜt* and the title combination *jrj-ᶜt wdpw*. The earliest monument mentioning an *jmj-r3 st* together with an *jrj-ᶜt wdpw* is stela Rio de Janeiro no. 627 [2419]. It is dated by a king's name to the reign of Senusret III. The main person on the stela is the *jmj-r3 st Jw-nfr*, while two people with the title *jrj-ᶜt* are mentioned at the bottom of the stela. Berlev (1978: 256) discussed the case of *H̱nms* who bears the titles *jmj-r3 st*, *jrj-ᶜt wdpw* and *rḫ-njswt* on different monuments. Berlev came to the conclusion that it is not possible to determine on present evidence whether the titles were borne by this official at the same time or at different stages of his career (compare the discussion of *rḫ-njswt*). However from the sequence of the *treasurers Snb-sw-m-ᶜ(.j)* and *Snbj* it seems clear that these are different steps of a career. The *jrj-ᶜt wdpw H̱nms* is mentioned on one stela (Cairo CG 20718) connected with *Snb-sw-m-ᶜ(.j)*. The *rḫ-njswt H̱nms* is named on a stela linked with *Snbj* (Cairo CG 20614).

The title *jmj-r3 st* is quite common in the 13th Dynasty, but only two stelae in the group discussed include a person with this title and its combinations in the main position:

Dublin UC 1360
London BM 903

Both stelae mainly depict people involved in food production at the palace. On the Dublin stela there are various people with titles connected with *jmj-r3 st* (*wdpw n ꜥt*). On the stela in London there are many officials with titles combined with *wdpw*.

Other stelae with an *jmj-r3 st* as main person:

Rio de Janeiro 627 [2419], dated under Senusret III; other titles on the stela: *jmj-r3 mšꜥ, jmj-r3 ḫnr, jmj-r3 pr, jmt-r3 st, jrj-ꜥt, jrj-ṯbw-njswt, jdnw, zḫ3w wdḥw, smsw h3jjt,*
Cairo CG 20716; other titles: *jrj (?)-ꜥt jwf; jrj-ꜥt wršw; jrj-ꜥt n pr-ꜥ3*
Tübingen 463; other titles: *jmj-r3 st, jmj-r3 ꜥḫnwtj, jmj-r3 st n ꜥt n ḥnqt, jmj-z3 n jmj-r3 pr-wr*

In the 12th Dynasty some holders of this title with longer title strings are attested. A person called *Jpjtj* was buried at Dahshur next to the pyramid of Senusret III (de Morgan 1895: pl. XI = Cairo CG 1486). It is highly likely that he served under that king. *Jpjtj* has the ranking title *rḫ-njswt m3ꜥ mrjj.f n st-jb.f* and the titles *jmj-r3 jꜥw-r3 njswt, jmj-r3 swt špswt-ꜥ3wt* and *ḥm-nṯr n k3 ꜥnḫ njswt*. The last title is also known from a seal (Martin 1971: no. 327 - *ḥm-nṯr n k3 ꜥnḫ njswt Mnw-ḥtp Mm...*). On another seal the reading of the title is not certain (Martin 1971: no. 1380a). In particular from the last title the strong connection between *Jpjtj* and the king and the king's cult seems evident. The *jmj-r3 st Ḏḥwtj* known from a stela in London (BM 805) might date to about the same time (Franke, Doss. 779). He also bears the title *jrj-jꜥḥ wdpw*, and has also ranking title *rḫ-njswt*. In a biographical phrase on the stela which is hard to read the *k3 ꜥnḫ njswt* appears again. Another *jmj-r3 st* with the ranking title *rḫ-njswt m3ꜥ* is *Ddw-nšmt*, who is the owner of stela Cairo CG 20052; his stela dates stylistically in all probability to the 12th Dynasty, but a more precise date cannot currently be given. From the evidence of these stelae it seems possible that there was one *jmj-r3 st* at the palace, who was directly responsible for the provision of food for the king.

In the time of about Sobekhotep III - Neferhotep I the title *jmj-r3 st* is often found with an additional expression (Berlev 1978: 325-327); see the following list. None of the following people and titles can be dated much earlier than Sobekhotep III, and none of them can be dated later than Neferhotep I. The appearance of this kind of title therefore seems to be typical for a short period in the 13th Dynasty. It even is possible that it is typical specifically for the time when *Snb-sw-m-ꜥ(.j)* was in office. The exception is the slightly differently phrased title *jmj-r3 st ḥstj* which is only attested for *Kmn.j*, who dates under Amenemhat IV. In this case it might be some kind of biographical phrase.

jmj-r3 st n ꜥt jwf

Rn-snb	stela, Cairo CG 20023 (datable about Neferhotep I)
Sbk-nj-pw	stela, Dublin UC 1360 (datable about Neferhotep I)
Nḥjj	stela, Louvre C 45 (about Sobekhotep IV)

jmj-r3 st n ꜥt jrṯt

Nḥjj	stela, Oldenburg 4403 (Franke 1983b: 161-162, 170)

jmj-r3 st n šnꜥw

Jmnjj	stela, Tübingen 459

jmj-r3 st n ꜥb-jḫt

Mbw	stela, Tübingen 459
Ḫntj-ḥtp	seal, Martin 1971: no. 1222

jmj-r3 st n ꜥt dqr:

Nn-ḫm.sn	stela, Vienna ÄS 143 (datable through the *jmj-r3 ꜥḫnwtj n k3p Tjtj* shortly before Neferhotep I)
Rn-snb	stela, Cairo CG 20117; reading uncertain (datable about Neferhotep I)
Nḫt	stelae, Vienna ÄS 181; Toulouse no. 1 (datable under Sobekhotep III)

jmj-r3 st wr n ^{c}*t dqr*

Rn-snb	stela, Vienna ÄS 143 (datable through the *jmj-r3* ^{c}*ḫnwtj n k3p Tjtj* shortly before Neferhotep I)

jmj-r3 st n jmj-r3 ḫtmt

Rnpjj.f	stela, Dublin UC 1360; Pittsburgh Acc.2983-6701 (*Snb-sw-m-*^{c}*(.j)*)
Ḥrj-w3ḥ	stela, Roanne 163 (*Snb-sw-m-*^{c}*(.j)*)

jmj-r3 st nt ^{c}*t ḥnqt*

Jjj	stela, Toulouse no. 1; Hannover inv. no. 2932 (dated by style and iconography under Sobekhotep III)
Nb-swmnw	stela, stela Dublin UC 1360 (dated under *Snb-sw-m-*^{c}*(.j)*)
NN (2X)	stela, Tübingen 463 (date ?)
Sbk-ḥtp	seal, Martin 1971: no. 1422
Gbw ?	seal, Martin 1971: no. 1349
Ptḥ-pw-w3ḥ	seal, Martin 1971: no. 524

jmj-r3 st n ^{c}*t t'*

Jmnw-m-ḥ3t	stela, Dublin UC 1360
^{c}*3mw Snb*	stela, Dublin UC 1360
Rrj	seal, Martin 1971: no. 856
Rḥw-snb	stela, Vienna ÄS 181; Hannover inv. no. 2932 (the two stelae are datable by style and iconography to the reign of Sobekhotep III)

jmj-r3 st n ḫntj

Znb	stela, Cairo CG 20334

jmj-r3 st ^{c}*q*:

W3ḥ-k3	stela, Vienna ÄS 135 (dated by style and iconography under Sobekhotep III)

jmj-r3 st ^{c}*q n* ^{c}*t dqr*

Jmnw-m-ḥ3t	obelisk, Durham n. 1984, Bourriau 1988: 66-67, no. 52 (Franke, Doss. 230)

jmj-r3 st wrt

Mr.tw.f	stela, Vienna ÄS 172
Mr-jtj.f	seal, Martin 1971: nos. 605-605a
Mḏt.sj-ḥtp (?)	seal, Martin 1971: no. 422

jmj-r3 st ḥstj

Kmn.j	box, Carter 1912: pl. XLIX; Fischer 1997: no. 323a (the box dates under Amenemhat IV)

wdpw jrj-j^{c}*ḥ*

The reading of the title is discussed by Berlev 1978: 275-6. Two attestations of it might date to the 12th Dynasty (but only *jrj-j*^{c}*ḥ*, instead of *jrj-j*^{c}*ḥ wdpw* - Beni Hasan, Newberry 1893: pl. 7; Deir el-Bersheh, Newberry 1895: pl. 8); it is not certain - because of the orthography - that this title is intended. If the reading is correct, the title *jrj-j*^{c}*ḥ* belongs to a group of phrases/titles which sometimes occur in biographical phrases of the 12th Dynasty and then become function titles in the 13th Dynasty (discussed in Grajetzki 2000: 214-215). *Ḏḥwtj* (London BM 805) bears the title in the form *jrj-jꜥḥ wdpw* at the end of the 12th Dynasty while in the 13th Dynasty the title is normally written *wdpw jrj-jꜥḥ*. The main title of *Ḏḥwtj* is *jmj-rꜣ st*. The two titles also appear in the same order (*jrj-jꜥḥ wdpw*) in the Dramatic Ramesseum Papyrus, which might point to a dating of the payrus not very far into the 13th Dynasty. In scene 10 of the Dramatic Ramesseum Papyrus a person with the title is mentioned and the following description is given: *there happened the taking of a jꜣm-tree and of bzn (natron) to the prow of a boat by the jrj-jꜥḥ wdpw* (Sethe 1928: 139). In the picture for the scene, a person with this title is depicted making an offering to a boat in which the king (or a statue of the king?) is standing (Sethe 1928: 246, pl. 3, pl. 14). In another scene the *jrj-jꜥḥ wdpw* is described giving the *king's offering* (Sethe 1928: 190). The picture for it shows the *jrj-jꜥḥ wdpw* in front of an empty boat. Sethe pointed out that the draughtsman of the papyrus might simply have forgotten to paint the figure of the king (Sethe 1928: pl. 7, pl. 18). From this source it seems to be clear that these officials had some function in close contact with the king. Among other title-holders mentioned in the Dramatic Ramesseum Papyrus are also some *rḫw-njswt* (Sethe 1928: pl. 4).

There are some stelae with several holders of this title (Vienna ÄS 172, Cambridge Fitzwilliam Museum E 1.1840, Tübingen 479). Many of the people from the stela in Cambridge are also known from other monuments, but always with different titles. One could speculate that the Cambridge stela was set up on the occasion of some kind of festival like that mentioned in the Dramatic Ramesseum Papyrus. From later sources it also seems clear that the *wdpw jrj-jꜥḥ* stood in close contact with the king. Is it possible that he was a person who for a designated period (one month?) had the right to be very close to the king; providing him directly food, while before and after that period he had to fill a "normal" office. The *jrj-jꜥḥ wdpw Ḏḥwtj* who bears this title and the title *jmj-rꜣ st* on his stela in London mentions the *kꜣ ꜥnḫ njswt* in a biographical phrase.

Attestations in the Late Middle Kingdom:

Jmj	-	stela, Tübingen 479
Pzšw	-	stela, Tübingen 479
Nb-jrwt	-	stela, Cambridge Fitzwilliam Museum E 1.1840
Nb-swmnw	-	stela, Vienna ÄS 172
Nn-ḥm.sn	-	stela, Vienna ÄS 172
Nḥjj	-	stela, Vienna ÄS 140 (reading of title not certain)
Rn-snb	-	stela, Cairo CG 20160 mid 13th Dynasty; Cambridge Fitzwilliam Museum E 1.1840; Martin 1971: no. 835
Rn-snb	-	stela, Cambridge Fitzwilliam Museum E 1.1840
Zꜣ-mnḫ	-	stela, Tübingen 479; Vienna ÄS 172
Sbk-ḥr-ḥꜣb	-	stela, Cambridge Fitzwilliam Museum E 1.1840
Ddw-Sbk	-	stela, Magdeburg
Ḏḥwtj	-	stela, London BM 805; he also bears the title *jmj-rꜣ st.*

jrj-ꜥt

Titles with *jrj-ꜥt* as a component, as well as the title *jrj-ꜥt* alone are attested from Amenemhat II (Berlev 1978: 235, on stela Louvre C 172, dated to the third year of Amenemhat II) and seem to become very common after this time throughout Egypt. A good example of the introduction and the spread of this new type of title is given by the rock cut tombs in Beni Hasan. Tomb no. 2 is datable under Senusret I and belongs to the mayor *Jmnw-m-ḥꜣt*. In the tomb several servants of the mayor are mentioned; for example numerous *wdpww* (Newberry 1893: 15). No one with the title *jrj-ꜥt* is found in the tomb. In tomb no. 3 at Beni Hasan, which dates under Senusret II or a little bit later, the title *jrj-ꜥt* suddenly appears (Newberry 1893: 45); two people are mentioned with the title. The title and its combinations are fully discussed by Berlev (1978: 235-259). Berlev records the following different title combinations:

A. *jrj-ꜥt n ꜣḫt*
B. *jrj-ꜥt n jwnn (?) njswt*
C. *jrj-ꜥt n jpꜣt njswt*

D. *jrj-^{c}t n jmjw-ḥ3t*
E. *jrj-^{c}t n ^{c}t jwf*
F. *jrj-^{c}t z3w jwf*
G. *jrj-^{c}t wdpw n ^{c}t jwf*
H. *jrj-^{c}t mw*
I. *jrj-^{c}t n ^{c}t ḥnqt*
J. *jrj-^{c}t n ^{c}t ḥnkwt*
K. *jrj-^{c}t ḥnkwt*
L. *jrj-^{c}t sb3jj*
M. *jrj-^{c}t n ^{c}ḥ*
N. *jrj-^{c}t n w3ḫj*
O. *jrj-^{c}t n w^{c}bw*
P. *jrj-^{c}t n pr jḥw*
Q. *jrj-^{c}t n pr-^{c}3*
R. *jrj-^{c}t n pr-ḥḏ*
S. *jrj-^{c}t n mḏwt*
T. *jrj-^{c}t n z3 n pr jmj-r3 ḫtmt*
U. *jrj-^{c}t strw*
V. *jrj-^{c}t n šmsww*
W. *jrj-^{c}t n šn^{c}w*
X. *jrj-^{c}t n qm3w*
Y. *jrj-^{c}t n k3p*
Z. *jrj-^{c}t n Kpnj*
Aa. *jrj-^{c}t ḏ3ḏ3wj* (for this title see Szafranski 1999: 102-103)

Most of these combinations are only attested a few times. The exceptions are: *jrj-^{c}t n ^{c}t ḥnkwt* (x10), *jrj-^{c}t n ^{c}ḥ* (x13), *jrj-^{c}t n šn^{c}w* (x16), *jrj-^{c}t n pr-^{c}3* (x40), *jrj-^{c}t n pr-ḥḏ* (x43)

It is an open question whether all of these officials were part of the administration under the *treasurer*. Only the title *jrj-^{c}t n ^{c}ḥ* is found on monuments closely linked with the *treasurer*. However, there is much evidence that even an official like the *jrj-^{c}t n pr-ḥḏ* was part of his administration (compare the common title *jmj-r3 prwj-ḥḏ* for *treasurers*), although the *jrj-^{c}t n pr-ḥḏ* is not mentioned often in connection with the *treasurers* themselves on monuments.

jrj-^{c}t n ^{c}ḥ (Berlev 1978: 240)

The title *jrj-^{c}t n ^{c}ḥ* is first recorded under Senusret III (no. 9). The title is found under Amenemhat III combined with the ranking title *rḫ-njswt* (no. 1).

1. *3ḫtj-ḥtp*	rock inscription, Hintze/Reineke 1989: 143, no. 494. He also has the ranking title *rḫ-njswt m3^{c} mrjj.f*. He is dated to the 9th year of Amenemhat III
2. *Jw.f-r-^{c}nḫ*	stela, Cairo CG 20149, 13th Dynasty
3. *Jbj*	stela, Florence 2512, 13th Dynasty
4. *Jmppw*	stela, Tübingen 479, 13th Dynasty
5. *^{c}nḫ-tjfj*	stela, Louvre C 249, late 12th Dynasty
6. *Wsr-k3-^{c}nḫ-^{c}nḫw*	seal, Martin 1971: no. 434, 13th Dynasty
7. *Bnr*	shabti, Arnold 1988: 36
7. *Rjs.fj*	stela, Cairo CG 20225, about Neferhotep I, stela of *Snbj* as *rḫ-njswt*
8. *Rn.f-snb*	stela, Magdeburg, about Neferhotep I
9. *Zj-nj-Wsrt*	stela, Frankfort 1928: 240-241, fig. 2, pl. XX.1. The stela is dated with the name of Senusret III
10. *Snb*	stela, Cairo CG 20235. The date of the stela is not clear and the reading of the title is not certain
11. *Snb*	stela, Leiden 53; Cairo CG 20075. The latter stela belongs to the *high steward Snb-sw-m-^{c}(.j)*; - since no filiation is given it is not certain if the people on the two monuments are identical

12. *Snbj*	stela, Vienna ÄS 171
13. *Snfrw*	stela, Heqaib no. 69, Zagreb no. 8, time of the *treasurer Snb-sw-m-ꜥ(.j)*

jrj-ꜥt wdpw

The title combination *jrj-ꜥt wdpw* (list of titleholders, Berlev 1978: 254) is quite common on the stelae around the *treasurers*. It makes its first appearance on London BM 831 (op. cit. no. 35), which belongs to a certain *Sbk-ḥtp*. The stela is dated to the 13th year of Senusret III. The next datable record of the title is on Louvre C7 (op. cit. no. 9), which dates to the time of the coregency of Amenemhat III and Amenemhat IV (the names of both kings are found on the stela). The stela Tübingen 464 (no. 20) and a box from Thebes (Carter 1912: 55, pl. XLIX; Hayes 1953: 245; Berlev 1978: no. 43) are datable to about the same time. The title holders seem to have quite a high position. Some of the title holders are shown on stelae as main persons. *Kmn.j* is depicted on the box mentioned above offering to king Amenemhat IV. He also bears the ranking title *rḫ-njswt mꜣꜥ mrjj.f.* His long title sequence is of special interest. He combines the titles *jmj-rꜣ st ḥstj*, *rḫ-njswt* and *jrj-ꜥt wdpw*. The title *jmj-rꜣ st ḥstj* might be some kind of biographical phrase like *ḥrj-sštꜣ n jꜥw-rꜣ njswt m ṯs ḫꜣwwt nb tꜣwj* (compare discussion of *jmj-rꜣ st*; Fischer 1997: no. 1004b - *privy to the secret of the king's repast as the one who arranges the tables of the Lord of the Two Lands*) which he also bears. From the last piece of evidence one might conclude that the *jrj-ꜥt wdpw* was in close contact with the food supply of the king.

Titles combined with *wdpw*

wdpw n ꜥt jwf (Berlev 1978: 279)

Jjw.f	stela, London BM 903
Jpj	stela, Turin inv. Cat. 1613 (date: Amenemhat III ?)
Jpj	stela, Liverpool no. M13846 (late 12th Dynasty ?)
Jtjj	stela, Chicago, Field Museum of Natural History 31647
Wꜣḏ	stela, Dublin UC 1365
Mꜣꜥ- ḫrw	stelae, Cairo CG 20556, 20666 (ANOC 50; Franke, Doss. 732. Date: shortly before Neferhotep I. Cairo CG 20556 belongs to the *jmj-rꜣ ꜥḫnwtj n kꜣp*
Ḥrj-jb	seal, Martin 1971: no. 1421
Ḥrw	stela, Cairo CG 20085 (13th Dynasty ?)
Ḥtp-n.j	stela, Louvre C 45 (about Sobekhotep IV)

wdpw n ꜥt ꜥqw

Snw-ꜥnḫw	stela, Cairo CG 20266 (about Neferhotep I - Sobekhotep IV)

wdpw n ꜥt ꜥḏ

Nṯr.j-n.m-ḏw ?	stela, Cairo CG 20225 (stela of *Snbj* as *rḫ-njswt*)
Sꜥnḫ-Mnw	stela, Berlin 7311 (Sobekhotep IV - *rḫ-njswt Rḥw-ꜥnḫ*)

wdpw n ꜥt ḥꜣm

Ḥrw	stela, Cairo CG 20565 (hard to date because of poor workmanship)

wdpw n ꜥt ḥnqt (see Berlev 1978: 280)

Jjj-m-ḥtp (jrj-ꜥt wdpw n ꜥt ḥnqt) Martin 1971: no. 47

Jwkw	stela, Liverpool no. 13846 (late 12th Dynasty ?)
Wꜥbw	stela, Dublin UC 1365
Bbj	stela, Louvre C 45
Mꜣꜣ	stela, Durham (ex-Alnwick 1946; Birch 1880: 280, reading after Berlev op. cit.)
Rn-snb	stela, Dublin UC 1365
Ḫwj	stela, Durham (ex-Alnwick 1946; Birch 1880: 280; reading after Berlev op. cit.)
Snb	stela, Cairo CG 20266 (about Neferhotep I)
Snb...	stela, Durham (ex-Alnwick 1946, Birch 1880: 280 reading after Berlev op. cit.)

Gbbw-wr	stela, Turin inv. Cat. 1613 (date: Amenemhat III ?)

wdpw n ꜥt tꜣ (see Berlev 1978: 280)

Jpj	
Jmnw-m-ḥꜣt	stela, London BM 903
ꜥn	stela, Munich 36 (Neferhotep I)
ꜥnḫw	stela, Louvre C 45
ꜥnḫw	stela, Cairo CG 20104
Ptḥ-wr	stela, Cairo CG 20104
N-mḥt-jb	stelae, Berlin 7311, Vienna ÄS 140
Snꜥꜥ-jb	stela, Munich 36 (Neferhotep I)
Ḥrj	stela, London BM 903
Ḥrwj	stela, Cairo CG 20266 (only *wdpw ... t* left, Neferhotep I)
Ḥtpj	stela, London BM 903
Ḫsb	stela, Turin inv. Cat. 1613 (Amenemhat III ?)
Snw	stela, Cairo CG 20266 (only *wdpw ... t* left, Neferhotep I)
Snb-jtw.f	stela, London BM 903
Snb.tjfj	stelae, Berlin 7311, London BM 903, Vienna ÄS 182

wdpw n ꜥt t -dqr

Jw-snb	stela, Munich 36 (Neferhotep I)
Jmnw-m-ḥꜣt-snb Nn-ḫm.sn	stelae, Cairo CG 20350, St. Petersburg no. 1081 (reading of title on the latter stela is not certain; dating of both unknown)
....-ḥtp	stela, Dublin UC 1365
Jr.wj-wn	stela, Berlin 7311
Pzšw	stela, Cairo CG 20160 (Neferhotep I or earlier)
Rn-snb	stela, Berlin 7311
Rn-snb	stela, Cairo CG 20718
Zšnnw	stela, Louvre C 45
Sn-snb	seal, Martin 1971: no. 1468
Snb.tjfj	stela, Turin inv. Cat. 1613

Titles in the combination *wdpw n ꜥt + ...* appear first in the mid 12th Dynasty in a tomb in Beni Hasan (Newberry 1893: 15, pl. XIX - *wdpw n ꜥt n mw*), but not very often later in this dynasty. On stela Turin inv. Cat. 1613 there are several people with this title combination. The stela is most probably datable to the time of Amenemhat III (see appendix III). The holders of this title clearly represent the lowest social level on the stela, since they are all represented only by their name and title and without a picture at the bottom of the stela (the same is true for stela Dublin UC 1365). The next attestations of this title combination all belong to the mid 13th Dynasty. The numerous occurrences of these titles in the mid 13th Dynasty might reflect the fact that more people were now in a position to record themselves on monuments. Another possibility is that the administration was reorganised and that as a result a title type which had been used before for a low-level official now became more important.

zḫꜣw n ḫntj

This is one of the most common titles found on the stelae around the *treasurers*, although the title itself is only directly linked with the *treasurer* on stela Cairo CG 20718. It appears more often on stelae of men with the title *jmj-rꜣ ḫtmtjw* (Cambridge Fitzwilliam Museum E 1.1840, Cairo CG 20023, London BM 903). The *zḫꜣw n ḫntj* appears in pBoulaq 18, where he receives orders from a *wdpw*. The latter operates in the inner part of the palace (*kꜣp*), while the *zḫꜣw n ḫntj* operates only in the outer palace (*ḫntj*) (Quirke 1990: 103-104). The earliest titleholder dates under Amenemhat III; most of the others are datable to the mid 13th Dynasty.

Jjj	-	stelae, Cairo CG 20023, Vienna ÄS 142
Jbj	-	stela, Cairo CG 20023
Jppj	-	stela, Cairo CG 20147
Pꜣ-tꜣ-Nḫb	-	seal, Martin 1971: no. 1716
Ptḥ-wr	-	stela, Cairo CG 20718

Mm	-	stela, Cairo CG 20718
Nfr-tm	-	stela, Cairo CG 20023
Rn-snb	-	stela, Cairo CG 20023, Cambridge Fitzwilliam Museum E 1.1840
Rz	-	stela, London BM 238
Ḫwjj	-	stela, Cairo CG 20023
Zꜣ-Sḫmt	-	seal, Martin 1971: no. 1344
Snb-sn	-	stela London BM 225 (Hall/Lambert 1912: pl. 10)
Snb	-	pBoulaq 18
Snbj	-	stelae, Florence 2506, Cairo CG 20231, dated under Amenemhat III
Kwjjt	-	stela, London BM 903
Tjtj	-	stela, Stockholm NME 18 (Morgensen 1919: 13-15)
Ttj	-	stelae, Cairo CG 20023, CG 20160, CG 20286

Remarks on the military and naval titles on the stelae

Several military titles appear on the various stelae discussed. In general it can be said that these are common military titles which are known from other sources and are typical for the Late Middle Kingdom:

Titles on the stelae of *Snb-sw-m-ꜥ(.j)*:
nfw (x2)
zj n dpwt-ꜥꜣt (x1)
šmsw (x2)

Titles on the stelae around *Snb-sw-m-ꜥ(.j)*:
ꜥnḫ n nwt (x3)
ꜥnḫ (n) ṯt ḥqꜣ (x1)
šmsw (x1)

Titles on the stelae of *Snbj* as *rḫ-njswt*
jrj-pḏt (x1)

Titles on the stelae of *Snbj* as *treasurer*
jmj-rꜣ dpwt (x2)
jmj-ḫt-zꜣw-pr (x1)
ꜥnḫ n nwt (x5)
šmsw šms (x1)

Titles on the stelae around *Snbj*
ꜣṯw ꜥꜣ n nwt (x2)
jmj-rꜣ dpwt(x1)
jmj-ḫt-zꜣw-pr (x1)
ꜥnḫ n nwt (x1)
ꜥnḫ n ṯt ḥqꜣ (x1)
nfw(x1)
ḥrj n tm (x7) (for the military meaning of the title: Leprohon 1985: 161)
sḫm-ꜥ (x1)
šmsw (x8)
šmsw n ꜥrjjt(x1)
šmsw ḥqꜣ (x2)

It is hardly surprising that the titles *šmsw* and *ḥrj n tm* are the most common on the stelae discussed, since both titles were in widespread use in the Late Middle Kingdom. The same may be true of the title *ꜥnḫ n nwt*. However, the father of *Snbj* bears this title and its appearance, especially on stela London BM 428 where it appears four times, might reflect some family relationship between the military people and the king's family. Some of the other occurrences of titles like *jmj-rꜣ dpwt* and *nfw* might be the result of the circumstances in which the stelae where set up; this might have happened because of an expedition to Abydos in which these people were involved. In such cases, they might simply have navigated the boat on which the officials travelled to Abydos.

Chapter 10
Groups of stelae

Remarks on the production of the stelae (full discussion see Franke 1994: 105-109)

In recent years, various scholars have researched means of grouping stelae into workshops or of assigning several stelae to single sculptors. A scholar who already arranged stelae into groups for dating was Evers (1929: 73-84). Evers was mostly interested in their composition. His observations are important and still hold true. However, his research in this area never received as much attention as his work on sculpture. Further research was carried out by Simpson who noticed early on that stelae from the same ANOC group are often very similar in style and can therefore put together on stylistic or iconographical grounds with confidence. However, for stelae from different ANOC groups Simpson gives only one possible example which might come from the same workshop or sculptor (Simpson 1974: 4, no. 25). De Meulenaere (1981: 78-79) identified and dated one group of stelae on the basis of the iconography of the roundel. There are some other groups of stelae which several researchers have collected in short notes in their articles and monographs (for example: Bourriau 1988: 48; Hodjash/Berlev 1982: 80). Marée (1993) has discussed a group of stelae of the 17th Dynasty and is preparing a major study of Middle Kingdom monuments from this perspective. Franke (1994: 105-117; Franke 2001) discussed in detail a local workshop at Elephantine which produced stelae mainly for Elephantine but also for Abydos in the 13th Dynasty. He also briefly describes some other workshops, which will be mentioned later. Finally R. Freed (1996) identified ten workshops of the early 12th Dynasty on several iconographical and stylistic grounds. However, it should be noted that the concept of the workshop involves unstated assumptions; it is as problematic as any other category. The prosopographical research in this book can make a contribution to the study of stela production, an aspect that cannot be ignored in any study of these monuments. The present chapter will therefore attempt to group some of the stelae around *Snb-sw-m-*^{c}*(.j)* and *Snbj*. However, the stelae will not be grouped in workshops and only very similar stelae will be assigned to single craftsmen or groups of craftsmen working together.

In general it is not easy to assign a stela or relief to one or more artists or craftsmen. It can be assumed that different people worked on one stela. A draughtsman made the outline, a stonecutter cut the relief into the stone, while a third person might have painted the stela (Franke 1994: 104-105). Only in cases where two stelae seem to have been commissioned at about the same time, can they be so similar that there is no doubt about their shared origin. In this case it may be assumed that the same person or people worked on the two objects. It must also be considered that in one workshop the same person might employ different kinds of layout, technique and iconography. Two contemporary stelae from the same workshop might therefore look entirely different. A good example is provided by the stelae which are carved in the silhouette style. It is possible to demonstrate that the silhouette style was very popular in the 13th Dynasty, especially under Neferhotep I and Sobekhotep IV (Franke 1994: 115). One might therefore suppose that all stelae in this style were produced by the same workshop or the same group of craftsmen. However, further study reveals that stelae in the silhouette style are attested throughout the entire Middle Kingdom (one early example: Berlin 1192 - Senusret I). The silhouette style was therefore in all likelihood a technique used by different workshops throughout the Middle Kingdom.

In the following discussion, two or more stelae which look very similar on stylistic and iconographical grounds are identified and discussed. They are called group A, B, C etc. Each section begins with a description of what is most typical for them and which iconographical details they share. From this starting point the stelae are either compared with other stelae which have numerous iconographical details in common with them (and might therefore have been made by the same draughtsman) or with stelae which share the same stone cutting technique. Although the stelae which are used for comparison might have been produced by a different workshop or different craftsmen, there is a high chance that they were made more or less contemporarily, using features which were popular at a specific time.

1. "Residential style"

Chart of connections between stelae in the "residential" style

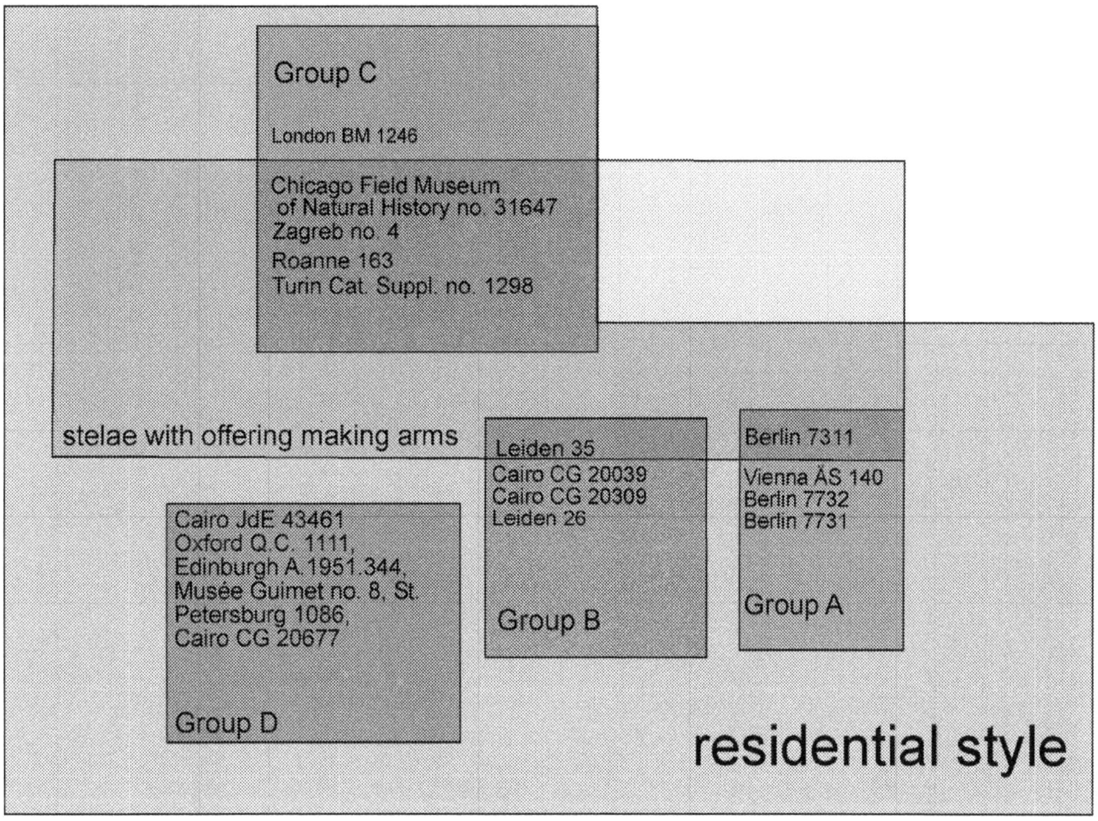

Group A

Stela Berlin 7311 and stela Vienna ÄS 140 (plate 3 and 4) provide a useful starting point for discussing the style and iconography of this group of stelae, which might have been produced by a workshop or a group of artists working at the residence or Abydos. Both stelae are quite well cut and belong clearly to the best quality private relief in the 13th Dynasty. The lines which divide the stelae into different parts are quite straight, especially when compared with other stelae of the late 12th or 13th Dynasty (for example: Cairo CG 20703, Vienna ÄS 96, 97, 115, 182 and many more). The details and the shapes of the human figures on Berlin 7311 and Vienna ÄS 140 are also well executed, though the faces of the women on both stelae show the same rough expression and look more like men's faces. In the roundel of Berlin 7311 are the two wedjat eyes, a shen ring and an east symbol on the right and a west symbol on the left. On Vienna ÄS 140 are two jackals, each of them placed on a shrine, and identified by inscriptions as *Wepwawet, Lord of Abydos*. Especially notable on both stelae is the carving of many details, such as the curled hair of the main figures and their clothing, a short kilt in two pleated parts with a longer garment over it. The relief is not very deeply cut and sometimes only the outline of a figure is carved into the stone.

Stelae with east and west symbols in the roundel

Although several features of these monuments are also found on other stelae, the east and west symbols in the roundel are not very common. In some cases the signs are depicted with an offering arm. All datable examples of stelae with the east/west symbols in the roundel belong to the period from Sobekhotep II to Sobekhotep IV. For this reason, it seems possible that all of the stelae with this feature are the work of a single group of craftsmen. At the very least it can be said that the west and east symbols in the roundel were very popular in the mid 13th Dynasty, and other stelae with this feature which are not otherwise datable might belong to this time.

Stelae with the east and west symbols in the roundel:

Berlin 7311 [without arms offering - stela of *Rḥw-ᶜnḫ*, official under *Snbj*]
Bologna KS 1929 [maybe datable under Sobekhotep IV]
Cairo CG 20147 [stela of *Rḥw-ᶜnḫ*]
Cairo CG 20445 [without arms - date?]
Cairo CG 20614 [stela of *Snbj*]
Chicago, Field Museum of Natural History no. 31647 [stela of *J3w-m-nwt*, official under *Snb-sw-m-ᶜ(.j)*]
Leiden 15 [date?]
Leiden 35 [stela of a draughtsman who worked under *Snbj*, Franke 1994: 115]
Roanne 163 [stela of *Snb-sw-m-ᶜ(.j)*]
Turin Cat. Suppl. 1298 [stela of *Snb-sw-m-ᶜ(.j)*]
Zagreb no. 4 [datable by style under *Snb-sw-m-ᶜ(.j)*]

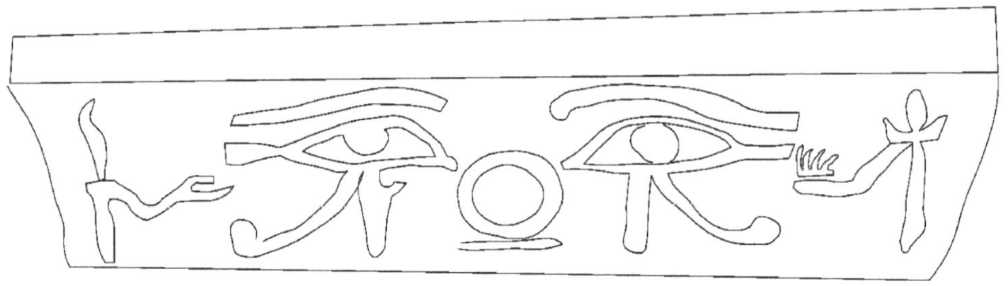

"head" of stelae Leiden 35

The stelae with the east and west symbol in the roundel are produced using two different techniques. Some of them are worked in the silhouette style, others in the more elaborate, detailed style already described for Berlin 7311 and Vienna ÄS 140 as group A.

Silhouette style

Stelae executed in the silhouette style (compare plate 2) have figures which are only cut in outline. The body of the figures is quite deeply sunk into the stone, and they have no internal details. This technique is only occasionally used, maybe for economic reasons: it must have been cheaper and easier to produce this type of relief. However, it seems that the style was especially popular in the middle of the 13th Dynasty. Many datable stelae using this technique belong to this time. This might not be coincidental. It seems that there was an increased demand for stelae in the 13th Dynasty. The silhouette style created the possibility of producing stelae of a higher quality relatively quickly. Viewed with the sculpture of the same time there is the impression that in the mid 13th Dynasty there was a strong tendency to stylise human figures, giving them a slightly geometrical shape. A good example is the well dated statue of *Šbnw* from the sanctuary of Heqaib (Habachi 1985: no. 70, pls. 164-65; for the date Franke 1994: 66). The extreme geometric stylisation of the scarab heads in back type 6 (Martin 1972: pl. 53) should also be mentioned

The range of quality of the stelae executed in this style is quite broad. While some of them seem to be of poor quality (Rio de Janeiro Inv. 639 (2429), Rio de Janeiro Inv. 631 (2423), Vienna ÄS 115), there are many other examples where the relief is well cut (New York MMA 68.14, Heqaib no. 47). The better quality examples seem to all belong to the mid 13th Dynasty. It is possible to assign some of the stelae to the same groups discussed above (group A), which produced also the stelae with the detailed hair. However, in general it is not easy to give many of these stelae an exact date.

Stelae in the silhouette style datable to the mid 13th Dynasty:
stelae around *Snb-sw-m-ᶜ(.j)*:
Cairo CG 20023
Cairo CG 20334
Cairo CG 20718
London BM 215
London BM 249 (almost identical to Vienna ÄS 9289)

London BM 252
Vienna ÄS 142

stelae around *Snbj*:
Heqaib no. 47
Cairo CG 20147
Durham 1941
Leiden 34
Leiden 35
Liverpool no. M13635
Moscow 5350
New York MMA 68.12

Group B and its relation to the silhouette style

This group of stelae is in many respects similar to the stelae discussed as group A. However there are some differences which make it necessary to distinguish these two sets (Group A and B) of stelae. Nevertheless, both groups have so much in common that they will both still be called "residential style". The starting point of our discussion will be stela Leiden 35. This monument is very important for understanding the relationship between the residential style and the silhouette style (discussed in Franke 1994: 115). On one side of the stela the *jrj-ʿt n k3p Snb.f* is shown sitting. This side of the stela is carved in quite an elaborate style, which looks very similar to Group A. In the cornice of the stela are the two wedjat eyes, a shen ring and the east and west symbols with offering arms. Under the cornice is a short inscription, consisting of an offering formula. In the main field of the stela is the owner, sitting alone in front of an offering table. Although the lines in this field are not very regular, the figure of the stela-owner is quite well executed and his garment is depicted with a pleat, similar to the one found on stela Berlin 7311. The other side of the stela belongs to the *nbt pr Sḏd-j3wt*. On the same side of the stela the *jmj-r3 wʿrt n gnwtjw* (*overseer of the section of stone cutters*) *Jnḏ* and the *jmj-r3 wʿrt n zẖ3ww qdwt* (*overseer of the section of draughtsmen*) *Jw.f-n-r3* are also recorded. This side of the stela is carved in the silhouette style. It is highly likely that both sides of stela Leiden 35 were produced at the same place and at the same time. This is evident from several other examples. Stela Leiden 35 is part of the ANOC 12 (Simpson 1974: pl. 21) with Cairo CG 20039 and CG 20309, both of which are produced in the same style. However, the prosopographical connection of Leiden 35 to the other stelae is not via the sides which are carved with the same technique, but through the side in silhouette style, on which the same people are mentioned as on the two Cairo stelae. They clearly belong to the "residential style" with the detailed rendering of the hair and the carving of the pleat of the garment. All three stelae mention the family of the craftsmen, who might even have produced the stelae for themselves (Franke 1994: 115).

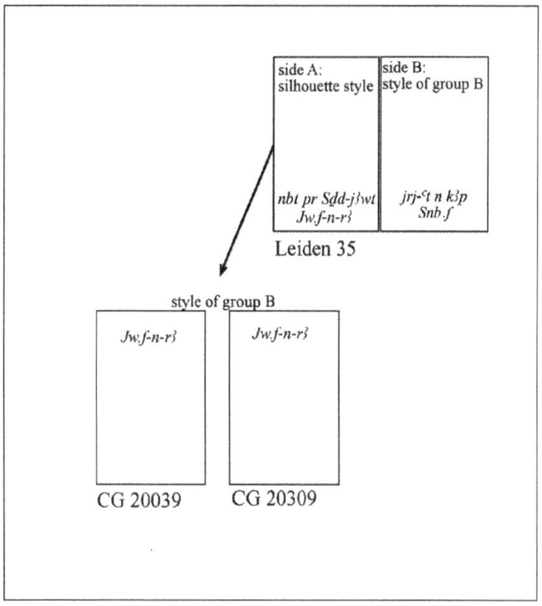

Another link between the "residential style" and the silhouette style is provided by stela Cairo CG 20147 which belongs to the *rḫ-njswt Rḥw-ˁnḫ*. In the roundel of the stela, next to the wedjat eyes and the shen ring, are carved the east and west symbols, with arms. Most of the figures on the stela are cut in the silhouette style, but one figure is carved in "normal" sunk relief. When compared with Berlin 7311 it is immediately apparent that both stelae have a number of features in common. The high-backed chair of the main person, the offering table and many hieroglyphs (compare the waterlines on the two stelae) are very similar. Both stelae have the east and west sign in the roundel but not on the same sides: on Berlin 7311 the east sign is on the right and the west sign is on the left, while on Cairo CG 20147 they are the other way round. The stelae might therefore have been placed in a chapel facing each other. Both stelae would then have been produced at about the same time as part of one commission. The same chair and the curled hair of the main person are also found on London BM 238 and Marseilles no. 223. Both stelae might therefore also belong to this group, although the stone cutting does not seem to be so good. The latter two stelae were clearly produced by different craftsmen.

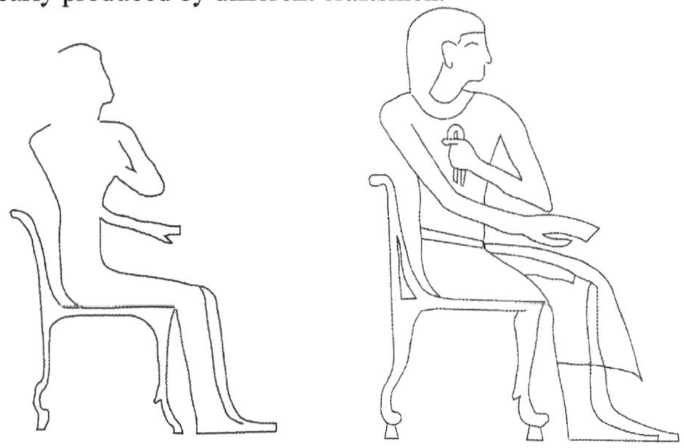

Rḥw-ˁnḫ on Cairo CG 20147 (left) and Berlin 7311 (right)

Group C

The starting point for the comparison of different stelae was the roundel with the east and west signs. Another stela with this feature is Roanne 163, which belongs to the *treasurer Snb-sw-m-ˁ(.j)*. On this stela the east and west symbols again have offering arms. Behind the symbols is a "t" and there is the sign for "land"/"desert". The stela again shares some features with Berlin 7311 or Leiden 35. The figures are carefully executed, though sometimes the proportions seem to be slightly awkward; for example, the arm of the offering man in front of the stela-owner seems to be too long. Once again there is the detailed hair, the characteristic feature observed on the Berlin stela. Nevertheless, the workmanship of the stela is different. The details of the figures are not very carefully cut and the faces in particular seem to be quite crude.

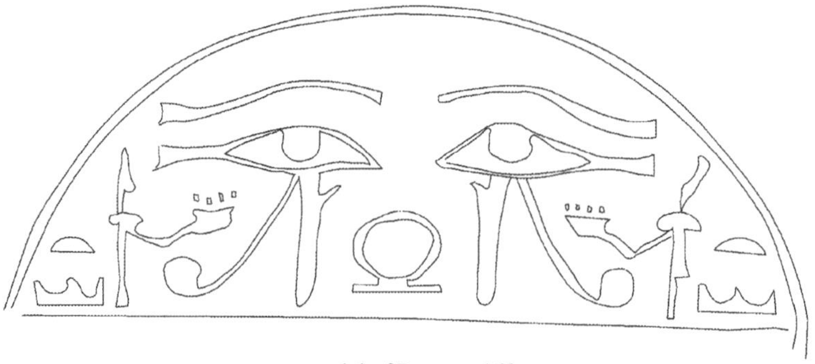

roundel of Roanne 163

Stela Roanne 163 is very similar in style and layout to Zagreb no. 8 (Franke 1994: 66 ascribes both stelae to a workshop in Abydos). The two stelae show the figures with detailed hair. The main person and the offering man are almost identical; one should also compare the over-long arm of the offering man on both monuments.

offering man on Zagreb no. 8 offering man on Roanne 163

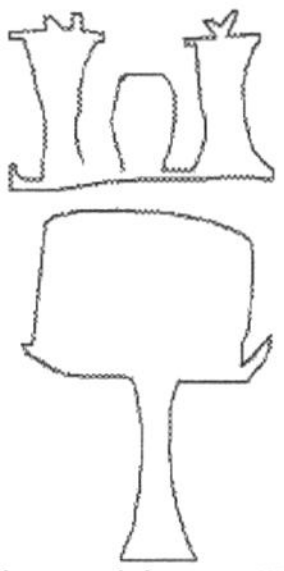
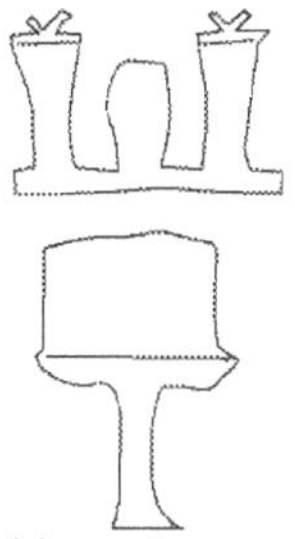

offering table on Zagreb no. 8 offering table on Roanne 163

The offering table and the three ointment jars over it are also very similar. Both stelae seem then to have been commissioned and produced at about the same time. This is confirmed by the persons named on then. Most important is the *jmj-rꜣ st n jmj-rꜣ ẖtmt Ḥrj-wꜣḥ*, who appears on Roanne 163 as the offering man and on Zagreb no. 8 as the main person. Finally, there is a third stela which looks very similar to Roanne 163 and Zagreb no. 8 - Chicago Field Museum of Natural History no. 31647. The iconography of the roundel is identical with Roanne 163. The figures again have quite detailed hair. Although there are no direct links between the people mentioned on the Chicago stela and those on Roanne 163 and Zagreb no. 8, the stela in Chicago is datable under the *treasurer Snb-sw-m-ꜥ(.j)* (p. 42) and therefore belongs to about the same time. The same is true of stela Zagreb no. 4, which is executed in the same style and uses very similar iconography to Zagreb no. 8 and especially to Roanne 163 (both stelae include the east and west symbols in the roundel, and the arrangement of offerings is similar). Finally stela London BM 1246 belongs to the group. This stela is prosopographical connected with Zagreb no. 4 (Franke, Doss. 175) and again shows the detailed rendering of the hair, which is even visible on the published drawing (a photograph has not yet been published).

Other stelae belonging to the "residential style"

Since it has been possible to collect some stelae around the *treasurers Snb-sw-m-ꜥ(.j)* and *Snbj* into groups on iconographical or stylistic grounds, it is also possible to allocate other stelae to this time, which are not related on prosopographical grounds.

Stelae Berlin 7731 and 7732 form ANOC group 74. Both stelae are close in both iconography and style to stela Berlin 7311 and might also belong to group A. The hair of the figures depicted as well as their garments show numerous details. Only the iconography of both stelae is different to the stelae already discussed. In the roundel of Berlin 7731 next to the wedjat eyes and the shen ring is a cup with a circle (incense?) on it. In the roundel of Berlin 7732 there are two jackals on shrines facing each other. Inscriptions behind them describe one jackal as *tpj ḏw.f* and the other as *jmj-wt*, so it is clear that they represent Anubis. The motif of two jackals on shrines is also found in the roundel of stela Leiden 26. In this case one jackal is called *first of the westerners, lord of Abydos*, while the other is called *Wepwawet, lord of Abydos*. This stela is also very close to Leiden 35 and to Berlin 7731 and 7732 in many details and might therefore belong to group B. The hair and garments of many of the figures are worked in some detail. The cutting and shaping of the figures is good but often a little bit careless in detail.

Group D

A related stela which is datable on prosopographical grounds is stela Cairo JdÉ 43461 which was found in Abydos and belongs to the *high steward Nb-ꜥnḫ*. The stela is well cut, the figures are well proportioned and the pleat of the garment of *Nb-ꜥnḫ* is depicted in equally great detail. From this point it seems quite reasonable that the stela belongs to the "residential style", which is supported by the dating of the stela under king Sobekhotep IV (through the person of *Nb-ʿnḫ*). In the roundel are the two wedjat eyes, a cup in the middle between them, and on each side three water lines.

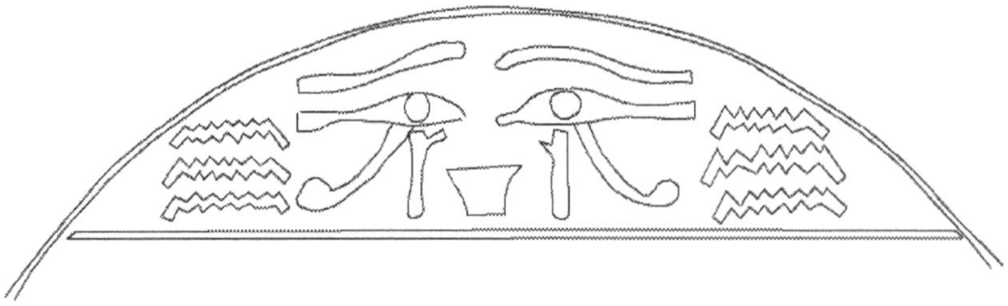

roundel of stela Cairo CG 20677

The same arrangement of the roundel can be found on several other stelae: Oxford Q.C. 1111, Edinburgh A.1951.344, Musée Guimet no. 8, St. Petersburg 1086, Cairo CG 20677. All of these stelae are also very similar in style and iconography. The main person is always shown wearing a pleated garment and sitting on a chair. In front of him is an offering table with bread on it and above it are some offerings on a mat. It is important to observe that pleated garments are not very common on stelae of the Late Middle Kingdom and this kind of arrangement of the offerings is also not so often found as one might expect (other examples: ANOC 19.3; Berlin 1204, 7311; Cairo CG 20075, 20093, 20104, 20309, 20556, 20666; stela Meylan; Leiden 8; Parma 177; Turin inv. Cat. 1620).

offerings and offering table on

stela Guimet no. 8 stela St. Petersburg no. 1086

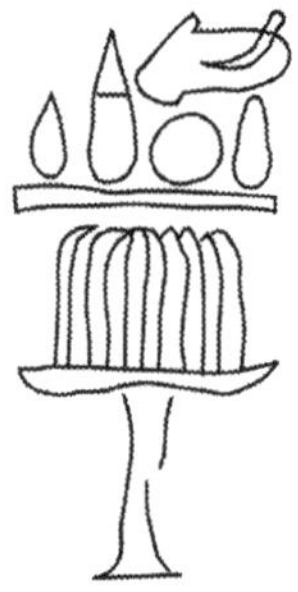

Two of the stelae (Musée Guimet no. 8, Edinburgh A.1951.344) include a long list of names. On stela Musée Guimet no. 8 the *jmj-rꜣ pr wr Nḥjj* is mentioned, who is also known from other monuments datable to this time (Franke, Doss. 331). His appearance confirms the dating, though there is the possibility that the identification of the *high steward* is not correct since there might have been two *high stewards* with the same name. The other *high steward Nḥjj* is attested on a stela in the sanctuary of Heqaib (Habachi 1985: 106, no. 91). His date is unknown. To end, it should be said again that stelae made in the "residential style" can still display quite a high level of workmanship. Stela Vienna ÄS 140 belonging to *Snbj* and stela Cairo JdÉ 43461 belonging to *Nb-ʿnḫ*, which are more or less contemporary, are masterpieces. A similarly high quality in private relief style would be reached again only in the early 18th Dynasty.

2. "Long bodies":

The elongated torsos of the standing and sitting figures are typical for this group of stelae. The upper half of the body is always a little bit longer in proportion than on other stelae. The workmanship of the stelae is mostly rather crude and the relief is always sunk. The figures are not very carefully executed, and the relief is very uneven; the arms and legs are also quite often of exaggerated length. It might be objected that the stelae of this style do not really form a group from one workshop and that all these stelae are simply monuments of poor quality. However, there is a chronological reason for arguing that they belong together: all datable examples belong to the time of Sobekhotep II (datable via the *vizier ʿnḫw* at the latest to the early years of Neferhotep I (stela around *Snb-sw-m-ʿ(.j)*). Crude stelae from other times present different characteristics (see for example Marée 1993).

The depictions of the offering table are also typical of this group: two or three round/oval offerings set against a lettuce or gourd.
The roundel of the stelae in most cases contains only the wedjat eyes, and sometimes a shen ring, with just a few examples adding recumbent jackals.

List of stelae which might belong to this group:

ANOC 61 (=Michaelides A and B); Cairo CG 20255; Florence 2503; Leiden 13, 14, 16, 33, 42, 50; Louvre C 16-18 (=ANOC 52); Rio de Janeiro 646 (2436); St. Petersburg 1063, 1064, 1075; Vienna ÄS 198 (?), 197 (?); Zagreb no. 6

3. Ankh sign in roundel
This group is briefly discussed by Grajetzki 2000: 165 (compare Franke, fortcoming). The key stelae of the group are Vienna ÄS 135, 163, Leiden 27, Leiden 31 and Hannover inv.no. 2932. On stela Vienna ÄS 135 the *king's son Snb* is mentioned who is known from other monuments to be the brother of king Sobekhotep III (Franke, Doss. 612). He is recorded with a full filiation and there is therefore little doubt about the date. The whole group might therefore date under this king.
The stelae have some compositional details in common, which are not often found elsewhere in the same combination.

a. One typical feature is an ankh-sign in the roundel (Hannover inv. no. 2932, Leiden 31, Vienna ÄS 135, Vienna ÄS 163).

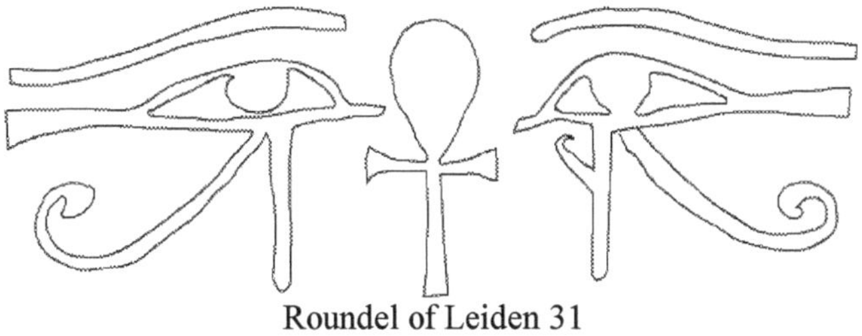

Roundel of Leiden 31

b. The writing of the hetep-di-nisut formula with the hetep sign and the "t" and "p" under it (Hannover inv. no. 2932, Leiden 31, Vienna ÄS 135, Vienna ÄS 163).

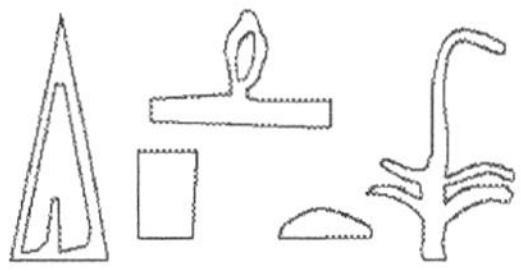

Offering formula on Leiden 31

The writing on other stelae is:

c. The arrangement of the offering table on Leiden 31 and Vienna ÄS 163 is very similar; note on both the dominant piece of meat (? or vegetable?) in the background.

Offering table on Leiden 31

Offering table on Vienna ÄS 163

On prosopographical grounds it is possible to connect two other stelae with the group. On Hannover inv. no. 2932 the *jmj-rꜣ st n ꜥt tꜣ Rḥw-snb* appears. On Vienna ÄS 181 the *jmj-rꜣ st Rḥw-snb* is recorded. The two people might be identical. On the stela in Hannover the *jmj-rꜣ st n ꜥt ḥnqt Jjj* appears, who is also the owner of stela Toulouse no. 1 (Franke, Doss. 16). This Toulouse stela records the *jmj-rꜣ st n ꜥt dqr Nḫt*, who is also attested on Vienna ÄS 181. These three stelae (Hannover inv. no. 2932, Vienna ÄS 181, Toulouse no. 1) therefore form a group of monuments which were probably set up in one chapel in Abydos.

Hannover inv. no. 2932	Toulouse no. 1	Vienna ÄS 181
jmj-rꜣ st n ꜥt tꜣ Rḥw-snb		*jmj-rꜣ st Rḥw-snb*
jmj-rꜣ st n ꜥt ḥnqt Jjj	*jmj-rꜣ st n ꜥt ḥnqt Jjj*	
	jmj-rꜣ st n ꜥt dqr Nḫt	*jmj-rꜣ st n ꜥt dqr Nḫt*

These two additional stelae (Vienna ÄS 181, Toulouse no.1) display a different iconography from the stelae first mentioned. They do not share the details in the roundel or the unusual writing of the former mentioned group. In the roundel are the two wedjat eyes and a shen ring. The hetep-di-nisut formula is written with the more usual orthography. However, both stelae share the following similarities, which makes it plausible that they were produced in the same tradition or even by the same craftsmen:

The sitting women on both stelae are almost identical

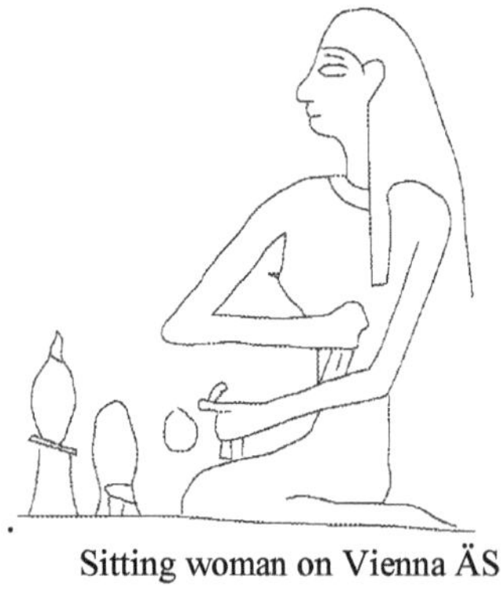

Sitting woman on Vienna ÄS 181

Sitting woman on Toulouse no. 1

The offerings in front of the people who are sitting on the ground are very similar, for example round 'floating' offerings are depicted on both stelae.

The nipple of the woman's breast is always clearly depicted, a feature not often attested on other stelae.

All of the stelae discussed seem to have been executed by the same sculptor. For all of the stelae the background and the outline are quite regular. The figures are only carved in outline; the background is only worked on some of the hieroglyphs. The form of the hieroglyphs is very similar at least on some of the stelae:

The Ka-sign with "loop" hands (Hannover inv. no. 2932, Leiden 31, Toulouse no. 1, Vienna ÄS 135, Vienna ÄS 163, Vienna ÄS 181); the "n" - water line on most of the stelae is a simple line with down-turned ends (Toulouse no. 1, Vienna ÄS 163, Vienna ÄS 181). On Vienna ÄS 163 the water line is sometimes as described here, but in the same text is also sometimes a wavy line.

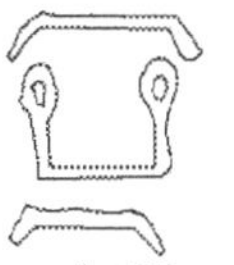

Detail from stela Vienna ÄS 163

It seems that stelae Vienna ÄS 181 and Toulouse no. 1 and the other stelae discussed belong to the same group of stelae but were produced by two different draughtsmen. Finally, stela Leiden 27 should be mentioned, as it might also belong to this group. The carving of the figures and especially the faces is very similar. The same is true of the image of Min, who is shown on this stela and looking very similar to the other pictures of the god in the group (Hannover inv. no. 2932, Vienna ÄS 135) particularly because of his crown. The image of Min on other stelae is totally different (Bologna KS 1911).

It is finally possible to add some other stelae to this group. As already mentioned, the group discussed is datable to about the time of Sobekhotep III. Stela Vienna ÄS 168, belongs to the *rḫ-njswt Snbj-šrj* who later became *high steward.* is datable a little bit earlier. The figure on Vienna ÄS 168 is quite well shaped, although the lines are not absolutely straight everywhere on the stela. The cutting of the relief is again simple. Only the outlines of the figures are sunk while the rest of the body - with the exception of some hieroglyphs - is not cut away. This kind of relief looks almost identical to that in the group discussed.

Other stelae which may relate to this group are Cairo CG 20015, CG 20101 and CG 20562, which all belong to the *high steward Jmnjj* (who was therefore in office before the *high stewards Snb-šrj* and *Tjtj*; his monuments date stylistically before both, who are well dated; compare Franke, forthcoming). Stelae Turin inv. Cat. 1627, Florence 2590 and Munich GL WAF 34 may also belong to this group. These stelae share the same careful cutting of the relief and the well-proportioned figures (though sometimes it seems that some details are not very well formed). The relief is quite often not true relief: figures are only carved in outline, while the body is not sunk. On the other hand, the face of some important figures can be quite detailed. All of the stelae have a roundel, which the two jackals, which are so common in the mid 13th Dynasty. Munich GL WAF 34 belongs to the *šmsw šms* (*the follower who follows*) *Nfr-nꜣ-jjj*, who also appears on stelae Louvre 206. The *jmj-ḫt-zꜣw-pr Ḥrj* (Franke, Doss. 309) is recorded on both this stela and stela Leiden 27 which belongs to the group under discussion.

Stelae belonging to the group:
The "core group":
Vienna ÄS 135, Vienna ÄS 163, Leiden 27, Leiden 31, Hannover inv.no. 2932

Other stelae:
Vienna ÄS 181, Toulouse no.1

Other stelae with uncertain relation to the group:
Cairo CG 20015, CG 20101, CG 20562, Florence 2590, Munich GL WAF 34, Turin inv. Cat. 1627

Pairs of stelae

Within the groups of stelae presented it is clear that there are many which belong particulary close together. It is surprising to see how many iconographical similarities are found between stelae which show the *treasurer* with an offering man and stelae with this offering man as the main person. After examining the appearance of these stelae, it is clear that they are very similar in style, iconography and layout. There is almost no doubt that several of these stelae were commissioned and set up at the same time and maybe also at the same place. These stelae always seem to form pairs. The custom setting up a pair of stelae of this type seems to be quite common in the 13th Dynasty. Many stelae which can be linked together by prosopography reflect the same system already observed around the stelae of the *treasurers*:

1. A stela of a high official with an offering man in front of him. 2. A second stela which belongs to the offering man where he is shown as the main person. The main difference to the stelae around the *treasurer* is that on many of these stelae the offering man is the son of the main person. The following list gives some examples:

Edinburgh A.1951.344, main person: *zẖꜣw n ẖnrt wr Snb-n.j*
Man making offering (his son): *zẖꜣw n ẖnrt wr Sbk-ḥtp*
Musée Guimet no. 8: main person: *zẖꜣw n ẖnrt wr Sbk-ḥtp*
Owner of Tübingen 458: *zẖꜣw n ẖnrt wr Sbk-ḥtp*

Berlin 7731, main person: *smsw hꜣjjt Zꜣ-Jmnw*
Man making offering (his son): *sḥḏ šmsww Zꜣ-Jmnw*
Berlin 7732, main person: *sḥḏ šmsww Zꜣ-Jmnw* (ANOC 74)

Bologna KS 1933 belongs to the *sḥḏ šmsww Sbk-jrj* . His brother the *jdnw n jmj-rꜣ pr wr Sbk-mnḫ* sits in front of him (*jn sn.f sꜥnḫ rn.f*).
The stela Bologna KS 1910 belongs to his brother.

Florence 2559 shows the *wr mḏw Šmꜥw Nḫjj* in front of his father (*jmj-rꜣ sḫtjw Ḫꜥ-ḫpr-Rꜥw-snb*). Florence 2561 and Cairo CG 20520 belong to *Nḫjj* himself (ANOC 32).

Toulouse no. 49.267, main person: *jmj-rꜣ st n ꜥt ḥnqt Jjj*
Offering man (*jn ḥr-ꜥ.f sꜥnḫ rn.f*): *jmj-rꜣ st n ꜥt dqr Nḫt*
Vienna ÄS 181 also shows the *jmj-rꜣ st n ꜥt dqr Nḫt*

Cairo JdÉ 43461, main person: the *high steward Nb-ꜥnḫ*
Man in front of him, in this case a singer playing a harp: *ḥzw Ṯnj-ꜥꜣ*
Stockholm NME 34 belongs to *Ṯnj-ꜥꜣ*

The interpretation of Leiden 43 and Leiden 44 is a little bit more difficult. On Leiden 43 the *singer* (*ḥzw*) *Nfr-ḥtp* is playing a harp in front of the *ḥꜣtj-ꜥ jmj-rꜣ ḥmw-nṯr Jkj*. In the second register an offering man stands in front of *Jkj* described as *his beloved son Nfr-ḥtp*. It is not clear if he is identical with the singer or if they just have the same name. However the name of the singer's mother and the name of the wife of the *ḥꜣtj-ꜥ jmj-rꜣ ḥmw-nṯr Jkj* are different. Stela Leiden 44 belongs to the *singer* Neferhotep alone.

All of the examples given are also noteworthy because the stelae in each pair are very close in style and iconography and might therefore have been produced by the same craftsmen at the same time. The question is how these stelae were set up. Did the person who commissioned the production of a pair of stelae put them in one chapel or did he place them in two different chapels? For the stelae which are made by a son for his father, it is hard to escape the impression that the father's stela was the only stela for him at Abydos. ANOC group 32 for example consists of three stelae (Cairo CG 20520, Florence 2559, Florence 2561). On two of these stelae (Cairo CG 20520, Florence 2561) the son appears alone and on one stela he appears making offerings in front of his father (Florence 2559). In all probability all stelae of ANOC 32 were commissioned by the son, who may have set them up in his Abydos chapel. They are all very similar in style and iconography. The father appears only on one stela as main person; however, he may never have had a chapel of his own at Abydos. The father-son pairs of stelae are similar to the treasurer-*rḫ-njswt*/*jmj-rꜣ st* pairs discussed in this book. On all of these stelae there is a sitting main person and another person performing an offering in front of him. However, the situation with the *treasurers* seems to be more complicated. There are several people attested, who are mostly not related to the *treasurers*, but who set up stelae for him. The questions arise whether all of the stelae were put in a chapel for the *treasurer* or in the different chapels of his subordinates. There are three broad possibilities as to where the stelae of the *treasurers* were set up:

1. All stelae were put into one big chapel which belonged to the *treasurer*. The stelae might have been put together in the chapel or they may have been set up separately around it. The stelae mentioning the *treasurer* might, for example, have stood inside the chapel, while the other stelae, which only mentioned the officials may have stood outside the chapel. A chapel, especially of a *treasurer*, would in this case have been full of stelae of people honouring their master, while some perhaps even a larger number of

stelae were placed outside. A good example for the way stelae and chapels could be placed around a big central chapel can be seen on the published plan of the Abydos cenotaphs (Simpson 1995: fig. 54), excavated by the Pennsylvania-Yale Expedition. Most of the excavated chapels are surrounded by other very small chapels, which possibly belong to subordinates. However, the two particularly large chapels excavated in the area (G5-2, G5-1) seem to have no smaller chapels around them. More detailed information about these buildings is not available, since some adjacent areas lie outside the section excavated by the Pennsylvania-Yale expedition.

2. The stelae were both set up in the chapel of the person who commissioned their production. This would mean that more or less all of the stelae which we know from the *treasurers Snb-sw-m-*^{c}*(.j)* and *Snbj* were not from chapels of their own, but from the chapels of the people working for them. Only the high quality stela Cairo CG 20459, showing the *high steward Snb-sw-m-*^{c}*(.j)*, would come from his own chapel.

3. The stelae were set up in two or more different places. The stela showing the son/servant honouring his father/master was set up in the chapel of the father/master, while the stela mentioning the son/servant alone and his family was set up in his own chapel. The stelae found in the Heqaib sanctuary on Elephantine which belong to people from the group discussed show clearly that this could actually happen. Since there might have been different ways of setting the stelae up it may never be possible to decide where a single stela was placed.

A further point should be considered. Some officials are shown in both positions: 1. As somebody who set up a stela for his master and who makes offerings to him. 2. As somebody who is the master on a stela, to whom other people make offering. If all of the stelae were set up in the chapel of the *treasurer*, the question arises: Where were the stelae set up for the people mentioned on the stelae of the servants of the *treasurers*? The answer can only lie somewhere in between. Stela Leiden 34 is of crucial importance for understanding this matter. The stela is decorated on both sides. On one side the *treasurer* is the main person, while a priest is the person in the second position. On the back the priest is the main person. He must be the one who commissioned the stela. The monument therefore appears, as if it were two stelae in one. The same is true, though not so obvious, in the case of the stela Heqaib no. 47. On one side is the *ḥ3tj-*^{c} *jmj-r3 ḥmw-nṯr H̱nmw-ḥtp* with the *jmj-r3* ^{c}*ẖnwtj ḫrp k3t Ḫ*^{c}*-k3w-R*^{c}*w-snb* standing in front of him. The latter person appears again on the other side of the stela as the main person. Each of the two stelae (Leiden 34, Heqaib no. 47) could evidently only be installed in one place and this might therefore be true for the other stelae which were produced as pairs.

The grouping of stelae discussed here is of course only one of many ways of arranging the scenes on one or more stelae in the 13th Dynasty. Other possibilities are:

a. Two more or less equal officials are shown on one stela (London BM 249, Cairo CG 20075 CG 20087, CG 20526, CG 20549, CG 20570 and many more examples). The same arrangement is sometimes found when a man and his wife are sitting in front of each other on a stela (Berlin 7731, stela in Meylan, Munich GL WAF 34)

b. Stelae decorated on both sides, which seem to be in effect "two stelae in one" (Leiden 34).

c. Stelae made exclusively for one person, mentioning a few, perhaps particularly close members of the family (Cairo CG 20459)

d. Major group of stelae showing a number of people in almost equal position. The most famous stela of this group belongs to the *king's mother Jwḥt-jb* (Ayrton/Curelly/Weigall 1904: 48, pl. XIII).

e. It seems to be not uncommon that a person set up only one stela for his master/*treasurer*. Apart from this person and his master/*treasurer* most other figures are members of the family of the person who commissioned the stela. There must remain some uncertainty as to whether these stelae really form a separate group, or whether they are the result of the uneven surviving record. It seems likely that many, if not all stelae in this category were once complemented by other stelae which showed the second person in the main position, but that these other stelae have not survived (Leiden 14).

f. Several stelae of one person. One stela shows the family, one stela the colleagues and a third may have set up for the man on his own (see the following discussion).

Almost nothing is known about the architectural context in which the stelae were placed. It is only possible to guess from other examples found in excavations. In particular, American excavations showed that parts of the Abydos cemetery were covered with chapels of different sizes (see the map Simpson 1995: 32, fig. 54, and in general O'Connor 1985). In some of the chapels stelae were still found in situ.

Bourriau (1988: 40, compare Simpson 1995: pl. 6B) published an excavation photograph of an Abydos chapel with a stela and a model coffin found in it. The chapel can be linked to ANOC 19, which belongs mainly to the family and the colleagues of the *high steward Nmtj-m-wsḫt*. The ANOC group dates most probably to the mid 13th Dynasty (because of the writing of the title *ḫtmtj-bjtj* with the red crown), although it is not possible to give a more precise date. Simpson ascribed five stelae to the group: Cairo CG 20087, CG 20100, Cairo JdÉ 39069, Bolton 10.20/11 and Manchester 2963 (Franke, Doss. 350; compare Bourriau 1988: 65, no. 50). On Cairo CG 20087 and CG 20100 the *high steward* is the main person. On Cairo CG 20087 he is sitting on the left side in the uppermost register and on CG 20100 the long offering formula is in his name. Cairo JdÉ 39069 and Bolton 10.20/11 belong to a certain *Jjj*, while stela Manchester 2963 belongs to the *jdnw n jmj-rꜣ ḫtmt Nṯr-r-ꜣw*, who is also shown on stela CG 20100 which belongs to the *high steward*. The stelae in Cairo come from earlier excavations and it might be argued that they belong to another chapel, since the *high steward* is only mentioned on these two stelae and *Jjj* is the main person in particular on the stela in Bolton and on Cairo JdÉ 39069, which were found in the chapel. However, beneath the ground in the chapel in question a model coffin was found with the name and titles of the *high steward* on it (Bourriau 1988: 93-94, no. 74). The allocation of the stelae of this *high steward* to the group therefore seems secure. Stela Cairo CG 20087 records the *ḫtmtj-bjtj jmj-rꜣ ḫtmtjw sḏm šnꜥw ꜥkj* (Franke, Doss. 192; Grajetzki 2000: 98, no. III.36). This person is also named on a stela which may not belong to this chapel (London BM 210). The stela London BM 210 is a monument focusing on the family of *ꜥkj*. One may wonder if this stela was set up in a chapel of his own, while he was mentioned in the chapel of the *high steward* because the *high steward* was his colleague.

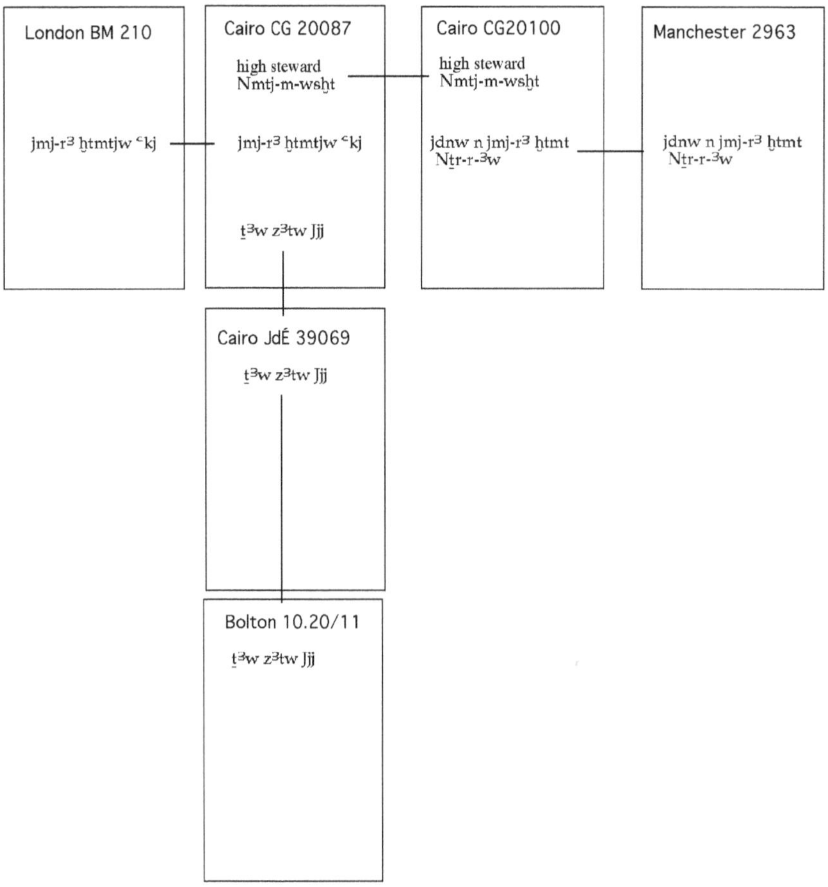

The architecture of the chapel of the *high steward Nmtj-m-wsẖt* is described as *a solid five-foot* (about 1.5 m) *square brick-built structure with a courtyard on the west and an enclosure wall around it* (Bourriau 1988: 65). Compared with the published plan of excavated chapels in Abydos (Simpson 1995: 32, fig. 54) the building seems to be of modest size. The question now arises how the stelae relating to the *treasurers* discussed in this book would fit into such a chapel, as one would expect a larger complex. Simpson (1995: 32, fig. 54: G5-2 or G5-1) published some larger chapels which may better suit the number of stelae which are attested for the *treasurers* and their subordinates. Examining the evidence from the stelae around the *high steward,* which centre on two people (the *high steward* and *Jjj*), it even seems possible that many of the stelae, which belong to the offering men/men in the second position were set up in the chapel of the *treasurers.*

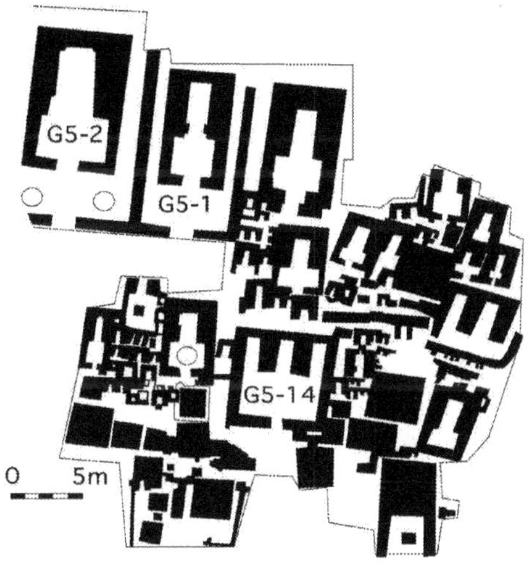

after: Simpson 1995: 32, fig. 54

In discussing the stelae which were set up by a son for his father, it became clear that the father might never have visited Abydos and might never have had a chapel of his own there. The stelae of the *treasurers* might therefore function in a similar way. For *Snb-sw-m-ᶜ(.j)* as *treasurer* and for *Snbj* there are no stelae attested which one might regard as monuments of their own. One may therefore argue that they never had a personal stela at Abydos and that they never even went there. Only their staff, especially the *rḫ-njswt* and *jmj-r3 st*, went to Abydos to work there and on that occasion set up one or more stelae for themselves and for their master. In the case of the chapel of *Rḥw-ᶜnḫ*, one might propose that Berlin 7311 was his main stela, which focused on his family. Vienna ÄS 140 mentioned the *treasurer,* the 'master' of *Rḥw-ᶜnḫ*. Cairo CG 20147 must also belong to the group, and one might wonder whether Cairo CG 20104 was set up in a chapel which belonged to the man offering on it (*jrj-ᶜt wdpw n ᶜt jwf Qqj*), though this is pure speculation.

Chapter 11
Discussion

Social levels

The preceding chapters aimed to show that the officials on the stelae discussed belong to different social levels. The *treasurers*, who quite often have the highest ranking titles *(jrj-pꜥt, ḥ3tj-ꜥ, ḫtmtj-bjtj, smr-wꜥtj)* clearly belong to the innermost court circle and to the highest administrative level of the country. The sources for the position of some *treasurers* even give the impression that he was second only to the king and had a position equal in influence to that of the *vizier*.

In front of the *treasurer* on a stela there is very often an offering man. This person belongs to a lower social level than the *treasurers*. It is therefore not surprising that many of the offering men are called *his child (ẖrd.f)*. In this position there is never another man with ranking titles, although there are some examples where officials with ranking titles are shown on a stela where a *treasurer* is also mentioned. These are the stelae Cairo CG 20614 (*ḫtmtj-bjtj jmj-r3 sḫtjw, ḫtmtj-bjtj jmj-r3 ḫtmtjw jmj-jz*) and Leiden 34 (*ḫtmtj-bjtj jmj-r3 pr wr, ḫtmtj-bjtj jtj-nṯr, ḫtmtj-bjtj jmj-r3 [ḫtmtjw] sḏm šnꜥw*) which belong to *Snbj*. For *Snb-sw-m-ꜥ(.j)* nothing similar is attested; the only exception might be the stela St. Petersburg, Hermitage 1084, where *Snb-sw-m-ꜥ(.j)* is mentioned alongside the *ḫtmtj-bjtj jmj-r3 pr wr Snbj-šrj*. The stela is exceptional because it is the only stela of *Snb-sw-m-ꜥ(.j)*, where he is not the main person.

List of the offering men in front of the *treasurers* /men in the second position after the *treasurer*:

Snb-sw-m-ꜥ(.j):

jtj-nṯr n Jtmw	(Leiden 14)
jmj-r3 st	(London BM 215, London BM 252)
jmj-r3 st n ḫntj	(Cairo CG 20334)
jmj-r3 st n jmj-r3 ḫtmt	(Pittsburgh Acc. 2983-6701)
jrj-ꜥt wdpw (z3.f mrjj.f)	(Cairo CG 20718)

Snbj

There are no offering men attested for *Snbj*. Only one person is called *his child (ẖrd.f):*

zẖ3w wdḥw	(London BM 428)

Although there are no people shown offering in front of *Snbj*, it is possible to make a list of the titles of the people who occupy the second position on his stelae:

rḫ-njswt	(Cairo CG 20614, Vienna ÄS 140)
jtj-nṯr n Sbk	(Leiden 34)
jmj-r3 ꜥḫnwtj jmj-r3 t3-mḥw	(Liverpool no. M13635)

In the case of the *treasurers* there are very often people with the title *jmj-r3 st* or *rḫ-njswt* in the second position. Interestingly, the *jmj-r3 st* is connected more often with *Snb-sw-m-ꜥ(.j)*, while the *rḫ-njswt* is shown in the second position on the stelae of *Snbj*. The first question which may arise is: Why is one *treasurer* always connected with one official and the other *treasurer* always connected with another official? There are two possible answers:

I. The titles *rḫ-njswt* and *jmj-r3 st* were held by the same person at about the same time. The different titles were put on a monument according to the function the official had on this monument (see discussion of *rḫ-njswt*).

II. The title *jmj-r3 st* is quite specific, especially with the *(jmj-r3 st)n jmj-r3 ḫtmt* - suffix which is often found in the context of *Snb-sw-m-ꜥ(.j)*. The real significance of the title *rḫ-njswt*, in particular in the Late Middle Kingdom, is not known. The only thing that can be said securely is that these officials seem to have a strong connection with the economic part of the palace. From the surviving evidence it seems possible that the *jmj-r3 st* and the *rḫ-njswt* had the same duties. It is even possible that both titles are in some way interchangeable. Sometimes a *treasurer* seems to prefer having officials with one title, while other *treasurers* prefer to take an official with the other title for the same duties. Since each title is mainly attested under two different *treasurers* it might even be argued, that a reorganisation of food production may have taken place maybe during the last years in office of *Snb-sw-m-ꜥ(.j)*. This is possible, but it should be remembered that under *Jjj-ḫr-nfrt* the titles *rḫ-njswt* and *jmj-r3 st* are both well-attested in his administration.

As already mentioned the officials who are shown standing as the offering person or in the second position on stelae belonging to the *treasurer*, are themselves shown on many other stelae as main person. On these stelae there appear in turn other people performing an offering. The officials who are shown here making the offerings are clearly yet another level further down in the hierarchy.

1. The following titles are attested at this level:
(the main person is mentioned first, then the offering man)

jmj-r3 st n jmj-r3 ẖtmt	-	*wdpw*
jrj-ʿt	-	*wdpw*
rḫ-njswt	-	*wdpw n ʿt tʾ*
rḫ-njswt	-	*jrj-ʿt wdpw n ʿt jwf Qqj*
rḫ-njswt	-	*wdpw*

Snbj, before he became *treasurer*:

rḫ-njswt	-	*wdpw n ʿt ḥnqt*

The following is a list of other pairs of officials - main person and offering man - which appear on the stelae discussed:

jmj-r3 ẖtmtjw šmsw njswt	-	*ḥrj n tm*
jmj-r3 st	-	*wdpw n ʿt*
jrj-ʿt wdpw	-	*ḥsw ?*
ẖtmtj-bjtj jmj-r3 ẖtmtjw jmj-jz	-	*zẖ3w n ẖntj*
ẖtmtj-bjtj jmj-r3 ẖtmtjw šmsw njswt	-	*(ẖrd.f) z3w-ḥnkt*
ẖtmtj-bjtj jmj-r3 ẖtmtjw šmsw njswt	-	*jrj-ʿt wdpw*

The title *wdpw* is the most frequently attested on the third level. With this title it seems that our investigation has reached the lowest social level recorded on stelae. It is hardly surprising that no stelae have been found with people with this title as the main person with an offering person in front of them. There is also no example of a *wdpw* in front of a *treasurer* or in front of another official with ranking titles. In this context the stela of one *wdpw* is of great interest - Dublin UC 1360. Here, a *wdpw* appears as the offering man in front of the *jmj-r3 st n jmj-r3 ẖtmt Rnpjj.f*. The *wdpw* is *J3w-m-nwt* who is also known from the stela Chicago, Field Museum of Natural History no. 31647. On this latter stela he is sitting on the ground. In front of him stands the *wdpw n ʿt jwf Jtjj* who is not making any offerings. Behind him sit two other men. Although the *wdpw J3w-m-nwt* seems to be the stela owner or the main person on the Chicago stela, his position does not seem as distinctive and separate as the position of the main people on the other stelae discussed.

The following social/administrative levels can be distinguished:

treasurer (with ranking titles)

rḫ-njswt

jmj-r3 st
jrj-ʿt wdpw

wdpw

From the positions of these people one gains the impression that there were three or four administrative levels in the economic part of the palace, which are visible on stelae. At the top there was the *treasurer*, one of the highest officials in the administration of the Middle Kingdom. The *treasurer* might have had a number of different functions. On the surviving monuments from the Late Middle

Kingdom mainly people involved in food production at the palace are shown, but this might have been only a part and maybe even a small part of his functions, in particular in the royal palace. Outside the palace he might have had a wide range of important tasks and positions. Under the *treasurers* there is often the *rḫ-njswt*. This title is again mainly connected with people involved in food production. However the title *rḫ-njswt* is also found outside the palace (e.g. in rock inscriptions) and some of these people seem to have had quite an important position, notably *Snn*, who is shown on stela Liverpool no. M13661 as more important then the *treasurer Snbj*. Officials with the title *rḫ-njswt* are never shown as the offering man in front of a *treasurer*. By contrast, this position is often occupied by an *jmj-r3 st*. This office seems to have had a middle position in the food production area of the palace. On the one hand they are the servants of officials with ranking titles and in this position are also called *his child*. On the other, they are important enough to have monuments of their own on which they are shown sitting in the main position, with other men making offerings to them. These offering men are sometimes also called *his child*. Officials with the title *jmj-r3 st* are shown as offering men in front of a *treasurer*, but they are never shown as offering men in front of a *rḫ-njswt*. Although their position was less important in rank than a *rḫ-njswt*, they seem not to have been placed in a hierarchy of command under a *rḫ-njswt*. This means that in relation to the *treasurer* the *jmj-r3 st* occupied a lower position than the *rḫ-njswt*. The situation becomes even more complicated with the title *jrj-ˁt wdpw*. A person with this title is once shown as the offering man in front of a *treasurer* (Cairo CG 20718), occupying a position similar to the *jmj-r3 st*. However, on other stelae people with this title appear in front of a *rḫ-njswt* making an offering (Cairo CG 20104). They are never shown in front of an *jmj-r3 st*. This means that there are three middle ranking titles in the palace, which seem to have quite a similar status, in particular in comparison to people above and below them. They make offerings to officials, but they can also receive offerings. A further investigation of the sources of the late 12th Dynasty shows how closely these titles are connected. There are two people with the title *jmj-r3 st* and the ranking title *rḫ-njswt* (Cairo CG 1486; London BM 805; compare the discussion of *jmj-r3 st*). *Kmn.j* even bore all three titles, although in a slightly different form (compare discussion of *jrj-ˁt wdpw*; Carter 1912: 55, pl. XLIX). However, all three titles clearly occupy different levels in the administration of the 13th Dynasty.

The lowest position on Abydos stelae is occupied by people who are sometimes shown as offering men in front of officials of middle rank. They generally have titles like *wdpw* and its combinations. There are only a few monuments known which really belong to them. More often these officials are shown on several stelae sitting together with other people who might have been in the same social position. It seems highly likely that these people still had an administrative function. The real working population would have been under them and is not recorded; it would not have been able to afford monuments with inscriptions.

Chapter 12
Remarks on the visual encoding of status of the figures depicted on the stelae

The main person on the stelae of the late Middle Kingdom is always shown with special attributes, in a different position or with a special garment. The main person is therefore always clearly distinguished from the other - in many cases lower status - people on the same stela.

The main person on a stela is often the only figure depicted sitting on a chair. All other officials on stelae tend to be shown sitting on the ground. The exceptions are the stelae where two people are shown as more or less equal sitting in front of each other (London BM 903, Tübingen 479, Tübingen 463, Vienna ÄS 103). Stela Cairo CG 20614 is remarkable: *Snbj* and *Snn* are depicted sitting on chairs facing each other. *Snbj* is sitting on the left occupying the better position, and he also wears a long garment, while *Snn* only wears a short garment. On Liverpool no. M13661 the two people mentioned on the stela are standing and facing each other, both of them wearing a long garment. However, in this case *Snn* is the one who commissioned the stela; he stands on the left and his figure is taller than the figure of the *treasurer*.

Stela Liverpool no. M13635 is divided into five registers, each with a person at both ends with his own offering formula. Although the same space is reserved for everybody there is a clear hierarchy. The *treasurer* is depicted sitting on a chair in the uppermost register on the left. The person in front of him is shown standing; everyone else on the stela is sitting. On stela Leiden 26 everybody is shown sitting on a chair: everybody is more or less equal. The same is true for stela Vienna ÄS 143, where all the figures are sitting on the ground, again, presumably, to show equality. However, the depiction of the people on this stela sitting on the ground might just be because of lack of space. A few stelae show the *treasurer* standing. On London BM 252 *Snb-sw-m-ᶜ(.j)* is shown standing with a sekhem-sceptre in one hand and a long staff in the other hand. In front of him stands a person without a staff, but wearing a long garment. The difference between the *treasurer* and the other persons is marked by their attributes. All of the people on London BM 215 wear a long garment. Everybody is standing on this stela except for *Snb-sw-m-ᶜ(.j)* who is the only person sitting on a chair.

While it seems that there is no fixed rule about the clothing and dress of the *treasurer* and other higher officials in relation to their subordinates, it seems that there are nevertheless always attributes and positions which reveal the importance of the main figure. The most important person is normally shown sitting on a chair, while the other figures are shown sitting on the ground. In the case where everybody is standing, the main person is depicted with some special attributes, such as a sekhem-sceptre and a long staff. In addition, a long garment seems to be superior to short garments.

Conclusion

For the mid 13th Dynasty two *treasurers* are especially well-attested by a range of different sources. The most important group of their monuments are the Abydos stelae. On these stelae many other officials working for the two *treasurers* are documented, creating a dense prosopographical network. The relationships of the people named on the stelae are very important for understanding the administration of the 13th Dynasty under the *treasurer*. At the head of this administration was of course the *treasurer* himself who might only have been directly responsible to the king (and the *vizier*?). Under the *treasurer* there were three offices who always appear in connection with him. These are the *jmj-r3 st*, the *jrj-ᶜt wdpw* and the *rḫ-njswt*. From their position on the stelae it seems that the *rḫ-njswt* had a slightly higher social status than the other two. The *jrj-ᶜt wdpw* was the lowest in rank of these three officials. From the people connected with them it seems highly likely that these three officials had a similar position and similar responsibilities in some parts of the administration, but there must also have been differences. The *jmj-r3 st* and the *jrj-ᶜt wdpw* always seem to be connected with the food production part of the palace (called the *šnᶜw*; Berlev 1978: 235-327, especially 319-326), while the *rḫ-njswt* seems not to be restricted to that part of the palace. He could be assigned different tasks and especially in the Late Middle Kingdom was often sent on missions all around the country. Some of these missions must have led these officials to Abydos, where the king initiated various building activities. These might have been controlled by the *rḫ-njswt*. On such occasions these officials set up stelae for themselves, for their families, and also for their master, the *treasurer*. In this context it remains unclear whether the *treasurer* ever visited Abydos himself. All of the monuments belonging directly to *Snb-sw-m-ᶜ(.j)* are from the Fayum area (Fayum, Dahshur). However, it should be pointed out that, of the two *treasurers* considered here, only objects from *Snb-sw-m-ᶜ(.j)* on his own are known. Excluding the seals, all inscriptions mentioning the *treasurer Snbj* were set up by his officials.

The appearance of the names of many high officials in so called 'expedition inscriptions' can be explained in the same way. None of these high officials need ever have visited these places (compare the mention of the *vizier* in Wadi Hammamat at about the same time - Goyon 1957: 101, no. 87). The same explanation might account for the occurrence of the names of king Neferhotep I and his family in the rock inscriptions on Sehel. The king probably never went there. The inscriptions were set up by one of his officials (in this case the *rḫ-njswt Nb-ᶜnḫ*), who wanted to honour himself as much as his king. However, the idea behind it might be that a monument mentioning an important person would attract more attention than a monument with only the name of a 'mediocre' official on it. At present it is still difficult to explain why there should be so many officials of the food production area on the stelae around the *treasurer*. It seems most likely that many of them also never went to Abydos. They might have sent stelae mentioning themselves to Abydos when their subordinates went there. Finally, some other stelae (Leiden 26; Dublin UC 1365, discussed by Quirke 2000: 236-239) might belong to people who really worked for a while in Abydos.

It was finally possible to identify a third administrative level under the *jmj-r3 st* and the *rḫ-njswt*. These people, often with titles combined with *wdpw*, represent the lowest social stratum visible on stelae from Abydos and other places. These people do not often have often monuments of their own. They still seem to belong to a social level where it was possible to have a career leading to the highest social levels (see the case of *Tjtj*). One might suppose that this reflects a high social mobility in the Late Middle Kingdom. However, although people with titles like *wdpw* are the lowest social level visible on monuments, there is no doubt that these people still belong to the highest administrative levels of the palace. The actual working population is barely visible. In our sources they are no more than the background decoration on some stelae of the Late Middle Kingdom and in the rock cut tombs of the Early Middle Kingdom.

Appendix I:

List of the non-royal (Vernus 1994) *treasurers* of the Middle Kingdom

1. Unknown position
   - *Jpj* seal, Martin 1971: no. 116
   - *Jk* Wadi el Hudi no. 61, Sadek 1980: 68
   - *Jtw* Cairo CG 23023 (about Senusret II-Senusret III)
   - *Nḫt* Cairo CG 20161 (compare Franke, Doss. 340)
   - *Nḫt* Athens, no. 6 (compare Franke, Doss. 340; Pörtner 1908: pl. II)
   - *Rdj-ḥ3* seal, Martin 1971: nos. 904-912 (Hyksos period ? 14th Dynasty?)
   - *Ḫntj-ḫtjj-m-z3.f* stela Petrie Museum UC 14487 (Kaplony-Heckel 1971; Stewart 1979: 31-32, no. 132, pl. 41. For reading of the title compare Franke. Doss. 472 with full bibliography)
   - *H3w* seal, Martin 1971: no. 915
   - *Ḫnmw-ḥtp* Cairo CG 20161
   - *Gbw* seal, Martin 1971: no. 1711

The *treasurer Nfr-prt-snb* (Martin 1971: no. 711) belongs to the early 18th Dynasty (and might be identical with *Nfr-prt*, dated under Ahmose, Helck 1958: 466).

2. *Treasurers* in the household of a high court official
   - *Nb-jḥw* Cairo CG 20561, Louvre C 167 (*high steward Jnj-jtj.f*)
   - *Nfr-wᶜb* Firth/Gunn 1926: text, 284 (*overseer of the harim Jḥjj*)
   - *Z3-Ḥwt-Ḥrw* London BM 162 (*great overseer of troops Jmnjj*)
   - *Sbk-m-z3.f* Cairo CG 20473 (*high steward Ḫrw*)

It might be an accident of surviving monuments but all *treasurers* who served on a private estate, worked at the house of an official who had the highest ranking titles (*jrj-pᶜt, ḥ3tj-ᶜ, ḫtmtj-bjtj, smr-wᶜtj*).

3. *Treasurers* at local courts

Qaw el-Qebir
- *W3ḥ-k3* Cairo CG 20549; Steckeweh/Steindorff 1936: 49, pl. 14a; statue, Turin Cat. Suppl. 4281
- *Sbk-ḥtp* Cairo CG 20268, 20342, (Franke, Doss. 589)

Assiut
- *Nḫt* Grab 7.1 and 7.4; (Chassinat/Palanque 1911: 53-114, 135-143, date: early 12th Dynasty?) *Nḫt* also bears the ranking title *ḫtmtj-bjtj*.
- *Wpw-w3jwt-nḫt* Hildesheim Inv. no. 6000 (Seidel 1994)
- *Ḥᶜpj-ḏf3* (tomb - Montet 1947: 132-133; Moss 1933; offering table - Cairo CG 23042)

Beni Hasan
- *Zkr-m-ḥ3t /Nfw* tomb no. 186 (Garstang 1907: pl. VII; date: 11th - early 12th Dynasty)
- *Ḫnmw* mentioned in tomb 2 (Newberry 1893: 17; date: Senusret I)
- *B3kt* mentioned in tomb 3 (Newberry 1893: 49; date: Amenemhat II-Senusret II)

Deir el-Bersheh
- *Nfr* mentioned in tomb no 2 (Newberry 1895: pl. XX, date: Senusret II-Senusret III)
- *Zp* mentioned in tomb no 2 (Newberry 1895: pl. XXVII, date: Senusret II-Senusret III)

Meir
- *Ḫnmw* coffin Warsaw inv. no. 142 144 (Dabrowski-Smektala 1977)
- *Nḫt* statues Cairo CG 433, 434, 436 (compare Franke, Doss. 340)

Qattah
- *Sḫmt-ḥtp* stela (Chassinat/Gauthier/Pieron 1906: 72-73)

Appendix II: The dating of stela Turin inv. Cat. 1613

On stela Turin inv. Cat. 1613, several people with the type of titles *wdpw n ꜥt* + ... are mentioned. The stela belongs to the *zḫꜣw wr n sḏmw Ḥrw-nḫt - great scribe of the judge Hor-nakht*. The title is not very common, but the few preserved examples date to the Late Middle Kingdom. On the stela the title *jmj-rꜣ rwjjt* also appears which seems to be more typical of the Early Middle Kingdom, although there are some attestations on seals (Martin 1971: nos. 264, 325; Ward 1982: no. 236), which point also to a later usage. The names of the people mentioned on the stela seem to be typical for the late 12th Dynasty (*Ḫntj-m-zꜣw.f* - Rosati Castellucci 1980: 46-47), though there are not many names which are securely datable.

Some other points show that the stela might date to the end of the 12th Dynasty, maybe even under Amenemhat III. The stela is very close in style to a stela in Meylan. The clear cutting of the figures seems similar on both stelae. They both have almost the same pattern in the roundel - different kinds of offerings - which is otherwise not very common. Finally, in the roundel of both Turin inv. Cat. 1613 and Meylan there is a wine jar which seems to be typical of the time of Amenemhat III (Bourriau 1988: 48). The Meylan stela is also not very reliably datable. Franke (Doss. 368) dates the dossier of the stela to the 13th Dynasty. However, the connection between the stela in Meylan in ANOC 68 and Cairo CG 20418 and the other monuments in his dossier is mainly based on the *jrj-ꜥt n wršw Rn-snb*. Title and name are too common in the Late Middle Kingdom to be certain that the connection is proved. The stela in Meylan might therefore not belong to this dossier or ANOC group. Finally, the stela Turin inv. Cat. 1613 should be compared with the stelae from ANOC group 26, in particular with stela London BM 557, which is dated to the 25th year of Amenemhat III. The two monuments share certain iconographical details:

a. the long hair of the men
b. the small beards which the men have
c. vertical lines of inscriptions over the heads of the sitting figures (in the first register of Turin inv. Cat. 1613 and in the second register of London BM 557).

These features are also not uncommon for stelae datable to other periods, but taking all the evidence together, they support a dating of the Turin stela under Amenemhat III.

Appendix III: Stela Berlin 7288 (height: 49 cm)

Berlin 7288 is a rectangular stela with a roundel at the top. In the middle of the roundel is an ankh sign, and on both sides is a jackal. The jackal on the right is lying on a shrine while the one on the left is standing on a standard with two uraei and an unidentified sign or object in front of him. The inscriptions next to the jackals described them as: *the northern* (right) and *the southern* (left) *wet*.

Under the roundel is the offering formula in three lines, which is quite unusual because of the gods mentioned: *Osiris, Lord of Busiris, the great god, Wepwawet, Lord of the sacred land, and the Ennead in the midst of Abydos*. In the main field there is sitting on a chair the owner of the stela, the *ḫtmtj-bjtj personal scribe of the king's tablet Iii-meru* (*zḫꜣw ꜥn njswt n ḫft-ḥr Jjj-mrw*) smelling a flower. The writing of his title with three "n"-signs is somewhat strange, but there can be no doubt that this title is meant. In front of *Jjj-mrw* is a rich offering table laden with different kinds of food. Under the table there are two pots on stands, with a flower lying on each. On the right side in the upper register *his beloved wife, the king's sister Seneb-si-mai* sits on the ground. In the second register sits *his daughter Anuqet-nefru*. The lower register is occupied by four people, each called *his son* or *his daughter*:

1. *zḫꜣw wr sḏmw rmṯ Jjj-mrw*
2. *jmj-rꜣ pr Jjj-mrw-ꜥnḫ*
3. *nbt-pr Rdjt-n.s-n.j*
4. *nbt-pr Sbk-ḥtp.*

The stela is not easy to date, but from the writing of *ḫtmtj-bjtj* with the red crown it is obvious that it dates to the 13th Dynasty (Grajetzki 1995). Some other features may even show that it dates to the second half of the 13th Dynasty. In the roundel there are two jackals: one is sitting on a shrine, the other is standing on a standard. This arrangement makes a slightly irregular impression. Jackals in the roundel seem to be quite common in the middle of the 13th Dynasty, but there are always two similar jackals, either both lying on a shrine or both lying or standing on a standard. Uneven pairings of jackals are not very common. They seem to be more typical of the later 13th Dynasty (Vienna ÄS 204; Rio de Janeiro Inv. 633 (2425). Only London BM 236 (ANOC 45.2, Franke, Doss. 102) gives a clue for the dating since the offering formula follows a pattern which is typical for the 17th Dynasty.

Translations of titles:

mayor	*ḥꜣtj-ꜥ*
high steward	*jmj-rꜣ pr wr*
overseer of priests	*jmj-rꜣ ḥmw-nṯr*
soldier of a town regiment	*ꜥnḫ n nwt*
overseer of sealers	*jmj-rꜣ ḫtmtjw*
overseer of the marsh-men	*jmj-rꜣ sḫtjw*
treasurer	*jmj-rꜣ ḫtmt*

References for published photographs of the stelae

Berlin 1192	-	ANOC 31.2
Berlin 1204	-	ANOC 1.1
Berlin 7288	-	Berlin 1894: 69; Berlin 1913: 201, pl. 6
Berlin 7309	-	ANOC 55.3
Berlin 7311	-	ANOC 22.3, pl 3
Berlin 7731	-	ANOC 74.1
Berlin 7732	-	ANOC 74.2

Cambridge Fitzwilliam Museum E.1.1840 - Bourriau 1988: 63-64, no. 49
Chicago Field Museum of Natural History - Allen 1936
Copenhagen ÆIN 967 - Jørgensen 1996: no. 82
Copenhagen National Museum – Morgensen 1918
Dublin UC - Quirke 2000: 223-243
Edinburgh A.1951.344 - Fischer 1997: frontispiece
Heqaib no. - Habachi 1985

Cairo
CG 20015 - ANOC 10.1
CG 20023 - Ghalioungui 1983: fig. 13 and 14 (the backside)
CG 20075 - ANOC 17.1
CG 20101 - ANOC 10.2
CG 20104 - ANOC 22.1
CG 20147 - ANOC 22.2
CG 20334 - ANOC 17.4
CG 20458 - ANOC 17.2
CG 20562 - ANOC 10.3
Cairo JdÉ 43461 - ANOC 46.1

Liverpool 13846: Gardiner/Sethe 1928: pl. XI

London British Museum
210 - Budge 1909: 96
215 - ANOC 25.1
221 - Hall/Lambert 1912: pl. 14
238 - ANOC 54.1
240 - Hall/Lambert 1912: pl. 32
252 - ANOC 25.2
428 - Peet 1914: 111-112, pl. XXIII (3)
504 - Hall/Lambert 1912: pl. 13
903 – Hall/Lambert/ Scott-Moncrieff 1912: pl. 47

Marseilles no. 252	-	Lattes 1992: 147, 192 (photo), no. 37
Munich	-	Dyroff/ Pörtner 1904
Munich GL WAF 34	-	ANOC 44.1

New York MMA		
MMA 68.14	-	Fischer 1996: pl. 25
MMA 69.30	-	Fischer 1996: pl. 21
Paris		
Louvre C 13	-	Spalinger 1980: pl. 8
Louvre C 39	-	Pierret 1878: 23
Louvre C 249	-	Andreu 1980: pl. XXXIX
Pittsburgh	-	Craig Patch 1990
St. Petersburg Hermitage	-	Bolshakov/Quirke 1999
Rio de Janeiro	-	Kitchen 1990
Roanne 163	-	De Meulenaere 1985: 78, fig. 1; Gabolde 1990: 35-38
Stockholm	-	Morgensen 1919
Stockholm NME 34	-	ANOC 46.2
Stuttgart, SP no. 12	-	ANOC 60.2 (pl. 42)
Toulouse 1181	-	ANOC 55.4
Tübingen no.	-	Brunner-Traut/Brunner 1981
Turin inv. Cat. 1613	-	Rosati 1988: 113, fig. 151
Turin inv. Cat. 1620	-	ANOC 54.2; Rosati 1988: 113, fig. 150
Turin inv. Cat. 1626	-	Rosati 1988: 112, fig. 149
Turin inv. Cat. 1627	-	Rosati 1988: 110, fig. 147
Wadi el Hudi 22-25	-	Sadek 1980: 46-52, no. 24, pl. XI-XII; Seyfried 1981: 62-73, Abb. 15-26
Vienna no.	-	Hein/Satzinger 1988; Hein/Satzinger 1993

Bibliography

anonymous
- 1994: Catalogue of Writing & Lettering in Antiquity 16. no. 20. London

Adam, S.
- 1959: Report on the Excavations of the Department of Antiquities at Ezbet Rushdi. ASAE LVI (1959). 207-226

Allen, T. G
- 1936: Egyptian Stelae in Field Museum of Natural History. Publications of the Field Museum of Natural History. Chicago
- 1950. Occurrences of Pyramid Texts with Cross Indexes of These and Other Egyptian Mortuary Texts. Chicago

Allen, J. P.
-1996a: Some Theban Officials of the Early Middle Kingdom, in Studies in Honor of William Kelly Simpson. Edited by Peter der Manuelian. Boston. 1-26
- 1996b: Coffin Texts from Lisht. In: The world of the Coffin Texts. Proceedings of the Symposium, held on the Occasion of the 100th Birthday of Adriaan de Buck. Edited by H. Willems. Leiden. December 17-19, 1992. Leiden. 1-15

Andreu, G.,
- 1980: La stèle Louvre C.249: Un complément à la reconstitution d'une chapelle Abydénienne. BIFAO 80 (1980). 139-147
- 1991: Recherches sur la classe moyenne au Moyen Empire, in: BSAK 4 (1991). 15-26

Arnold, F.
- 1990: The Control Notes and Team Marks. The South Cemeteries of Lisht II. New York

Arnold, Dorothea
- 1991a: Amenemhat I and the Early Twelfth Dynasty at Thebes. MMJ 26 (1991), 5-47

Arnold, Dieter
- 1988. The South Cemeteries of Lisht I. The Pyramid of Senwosret. New York 1988
- 1991b: El-Lischt. Nachuntersuchungen an einem alten Grabungsort. Antike Welt 3 (1991). 154-160
- 1996: Two New Mastabas of the Twelfth Dynasty at Dahshur. Egyptian Archaeology 9 (1996). 23-25

Ayrton, E.R., Currelly. C.T., Weigall. A.E.P.
- 1904: Abydos III. EES 25. London

Baud, Michel
- 1999: Famille royal et pouvoir sous l'Ancien Empire égyptien BdÉ 126/1. Cairo

von Beckerath, J.
- 1964: Untersuchungen zur politischen Geschichte der Zweiten Zwischenzeit in Ägypten. Ägyptologische Forschungen 23. Glückstadt

Ben-Tor, D.
- Seals and Kings. With contributions by S. J. Allen and J.P. Allen. BASOR 315. August 1999. 47-74

Berlev, O.
- 1971: Les prétendus 'citadins' au Moyen Empire. RdÉ 23 (1971). 23-48
- 1972b: Трудовое население Егпта в эпоху Среднего царства. Moskow
- 1974a: A Contemporary of King Sewaḥ-en-Re^{c}. JEA 60 (1974). 106-113
- 1974b: Стела вюрцбургского музея (xiii династия). Палесмнский Сборник (Palestinskii sbornik) 25 (88) Leningrad, 1974, 26-31
- 1978: Обшетвенные отношения в Египте эпохи Среднего царства. Moscow

Berlin
- 1894: Ausführliches Verzeichniss der Aegyptischen Altertümer, Gipsabgüsse und Papyrus. Berlin
- 1913: Aegyptische Inschriften aus den königlichen Museen zu Berlin. I: Inschriften von der ältesten Zeit bis zum Ende der Hyksoszeit. Leipzig

Birch, S.
- 1880: Catalogue of the Collection of Egyptian Antiquities at Alnwick Castle. London

Blackman , A.M.
- 1931: The Stele of Thethi, Brit. Museum No. 614, JEA 17 (1931), 55-61

Blumenthal, E.
- 1977: Die Textgattung Expeditionsbericht in Ägypten. in: Fragen an die Altägyptische Literatur. Studien zum Gedenken an Eberhard Otto. Edited by Jan Assmann. Wiesbaden. 85-118

Bolshakov, A. O.; Quirke, S. G.
- 1999: The Middle Kingdom Stelae in the Hermitage. Utrecht/Paris

Bosticco, S.
- 1959: Museo Archeologico di Firenze. Le stele egiziane dall`antico al nuovo regno. Rome

Brack, A.
- 1984: Diskussionsbeitrag zu dem Titel *ẖkrt njswt*. SAK 11 (1984). 183-186

Bresciani, E.
- 1979: Un Edificio di Kha-anekh-Ra Sobek-hotep ad Abido (MSS Acerbi, Biblioteca comunale di Mantova). Egitto e vicino oriente 2 (1979). 1-20

Brunner-Traut, E.; Brunner, H.
- 1981: Die Ägyptische Sammlung der Universität Tübingen. Mainz

Bourriau, J.
- 1982: Three monuments from Memphis in the Fitzwilliam Museum. JEA 68 (1982). 51-59
- 1988: Pharaohs and Mortals. Cambridge

Budge, E.A.W.
- 1909: British Museum. A Guide to the Egyptian Galleries (Sculpture). London

Carter, H.
- 1912: Five Years' Explorations at Thebes. Oxford

Chassinat, MM. É.; Gauthier, H.; Pieron H.
- 1906: Fouilles de Qattah. MIFAO 14. Cairo

Chassinat, MM. É.; Palanque, Ch.
- 1911: Une campagne de fouilles dans la nécropole d'Assiout, MIFAO 24. Cairo

Clère, J.J.
-1982: La stèle de Sânkhptah, chambellan du roi Râḥotep. JEA 68 (1982). 60-68

Craig Patch, D.
- 1990: Reflections of Greatness. Ancient Egypt at the Carnegie Museum of Natural History. Pittsburgh

Dabrowski-Smektała, E.
- 1977: New Parallels to the Spell 398 of the Coffin Texts, Ägypten und Kusch, [Fritz Hintze zum 60. Geburtstag], Berlin. 115-120

Delange, E.
- 1987: Catalogue de statues égyptiennes du Moyen Empire. Paris

Dodson. A./Janssen J.J.
- 1989: A Theban Tomb and its Tenants. JEA 75 (1989). 125-138

Donohue, V.A.
- 1966: Bolton Museum and Art Gallery. The Egyptian Collection. Oxford

Downes, D.
- 1974: The Excavations at Esna 1905-1906. Warminster

Doxey, D. M.
- 1998: Egyptian Non-Royal Epithets in the Middle Kingdom. Probleme der Ägyptologie 12. Leiden. Boston. Cologne

Drenkhahn, R.
- 1976: Bemerkungen zu dem Titel *ḫkr.t nswt*. SAK 4 (1976). 59-67

Dyroff K./ Pörtner, B.
- 1904: Aegyptische Grabsteine und Denksteine aus süddeutschen Sammlungen II: München. Strassburg i.E.

Engelmann-von Carnap, B.
- 1999: Die Struktur des thebanischen Beamtenfriedhofs in der ersten Hälfte der 18. Dynastie. ADAIK 15. Berlin

Evers, H.G.
- 1929: Staat aus dem Stein. II. Munich

Fay, B.
- 1988: Amenemhat V – Vienna/Assuan. MDAIK 44 (1988). 67-77
- 1993: Custodian of the Seal, Mentuhotep. GM 133 (1993). 19-35
- 1996a: The Louvre Sphinx and Royal Sculpture from the Reign of Amenemhat II. Mainz
- 1996b: The 'Abydos Princess'. MDAIK 52 (1996). 115-141

Firth, C.M./Gunn, B.
- 1926: Excavations at Saqqara, Teti Pyramid Cemeteries, Cairo

Fischer, H. G.
- 1996: Egyptian Studies III. Varia Nova. New York
- 1997: Egyptian Titles of the Middle Kingdom. A Supplement to Wm. Ward's Index. Second Edition. New York

Franke, D.
- 1982: Nachtrag zum "Richter der Arbeiter" (*Sḏmj Šnʿw*), GM 53, 1982, 15-21., GM 54 (1982), 51-52
- 1983a: Altägyptische Verwandtschaftsbezeichungen im Mittleren Reich. Hamburger Ägyptologische Studien 3
- 1983b: Die Stele Inv. Nr. 4403 im Landesmuseum in Oldenburg. Zur Lebensmittelproduktion in der 13. Dynastie. SAK 10 (1983). 157-178
- 1984: Personendaten aus dem Mittleren Reich. Ägyptologische Abhandlungen 41. Wiesbaden
- 1988: Die Hockerstatue des Sonbso-mei in Leiden und Statuen mit nach oben gerichteten Handflächen. OMRO 68 (1988). 59-76
- 1990: Review of W. A. Ward. Essays on Feminine Titles of the Middle Kingdom and Related Subjects. JEA 76 (1990). 228-232
- 1991: The career of Khnumhotep III of Beni Hasan and the so-called "decline of the nomarchs", in Middle Kingdom Studies. edited by S. Quirke. New Malden. 51-67
- 1994: Das Heiligtum des Heqaib auf Elephantine. SAGA 9. Heidelberg
- 2001: Drei neue Stelen des Mittleren Reiches von Elephantine. MDAIK 57 (2001). 15-34
- forthcoming: review of Grajetzki 2000

Frankfort, H.,
-1928: The Cemeteries of Abydos: Work of the Season 1925-26, JEA 14 (1928), 235-245

Freed, R.
- 1996: Stela Workshops of Early Dynasty 12, in: Studies in Honor of William Kelly Simpson. Edited by Peter der Manuelian. Boston. 297-336

Gabolde, M. (editor).
– 1990 Catalogue des Antiquitiés Êgyptiennes du Musée Joseph Déchelette. Roanne

Gardiner, A. H.; Peet, T. E.; Černý, J.
- 1955: The Inscriptions of Sinai II. London

Gardiner, A. H.; Sethe, K.
- 1928: Egyptian Letters to the Dead. London

Garstang, J.
- 1901: El Arabah. BASAE 6. London
- 1907: The Burial Customs of Ancient Egypt. London

Gauthier, M. H.
- 1918: Le titre (imi-ra akhnouti) et ses acceptions diverses. BIFAO XV (1918). 196-206

Gautier, MM. J.-E. /Jéquier, G.
- 1902: Mémoire sur les fouilles de Licht. MIFAO 6

Gayet, A.J.
- 1889: Musée du Louvre. Stèles de la XIIe Dynastie. Paris

Ghaulioungui, P., M.D., F.R.C.P.,
- 1983: The Physicians of Pharaonic Egypt. Mainz

Goedicke, H.
- 1977: A new Hyksos inscription. SSEA Newsletter 7. no. 4. August 1977. 10-12

Goyon, G.
- 1957: Nouvelles inscriptions rupêtres du Wadi Hammamat. Paris

Grajetzki, W.
- 1995: Der Schatzmeister Amenhotep und eine weitere Datierungshilfe für Denkmäler des Mittleren Reiches. BSEG 19 (1995). 5-11
- 2000: Die höchsten Beamten der ägyptischen Zentralverwaltung zur Zeit des Mittleren Reiches. Schriften zur Ägyptologie A2. Berlin

Griffith, F.Ll.
-1898: The Petrie Papyri: Hieratic Papyri from Kahun and Gurob. London

Habachi, L.
-1981: New Light on the Neferhotep I Family, as Revealed by their Inscriptions in the Cataract Area. Studies in Ancient Egypt, the Aegean, and the Sudan. Essays in honor of Dows Dunham on the occasion of his 90th birthday. June 1, 1980. Boston. 77-81
- 1985: Labib Habachi. Elephantine IV. The Sanctuary of Heqaib. AV 33. Mainz

Hall. H.R.; Lambert. E.J.
- 1912: Hieroglyphic Texts from Egyptian Stelae &c. in the British Museum III. London

Hall. H.R.; Lambert, E.J.; Scott-Moncrieff, P.D.
- 1912: Hieroglyphic Texts from Egyptian Stelae &c. in the British Museum II. London

Hayes, William C.
- 1947: Ḥoremkhauef of Nekhen and His Trip to Iṯ-towe. JEA 33 (1947). 3-11
-1953: The Scepter of Egypt. I. New York

Hein, I.; Satzinger, H.
- 1988: Stelen des Mittleren Reiches I. CAA Kunsthistorisches Museum Wien 4
- 1993: Stelen des Mittleren Reiches II. CAA Kunsthistorisches Museum Wien 7

Helck, W.
- 1958: Zur Verwaltung des Mittleren und Neuen Reiches. Leiden-Köln
- 1975: Historisch-Biographische Texte der 2. Zwischenzeit und neue Texte der 18. Dynastie. KÄT

Hintze, F.; Reinecke, W. F.
- 1989: Felsinschriften aus dem sudanesischen Nubien. Berlin

Hodjash, S.; Berlev. O.
- 1982: The Egyptian Reliefs and Stelae in the Pushkin Museum of Fine Arts, Moscow. Leningrad

James, T.G.H.
- 1974: Corpus of Hieroglyphic Inscriptions in the Brooklyn Museum I, From Dynasty I to the End of Dynasty XVIII. Oxford

Jones, D.
- 2000: An Index of Ancient Egyptian Titles, Epithets and Phrases of the Old Kingdom. Oxford

Jørgensen, M.
- 1996: Catalogue. Egypt I (3000-1555 B.C.). Ny Carlsberg Glytotek. Copenhagen

Kahl, J.
- 1999: Siut-Theben. Zur Wertschätzung von Tradition im alten Ägypten. Probleme der Ägyptologie 13, Leiden/Boston/Köln

Kaplony-Heckel, U.
- 1971: Eine hieratische Stele des Mittleren Reiches (University College London, In. Nr. 14487). JEA 57 (1971). 20-27

Keel, O.
- 1997: Corpus der Stempelsiegel-Amulette aus Palästina/Israel. I. Von den Anfängen bis zur Perserzeit. Katalog. Band I: Von Tell Abu Farağ bis ʹAtlit. OBO 13. Series Archaeologica. Freiburg

Kemp, B. J.
- 1968: The Osiris Temple of Abydos. MDAIK 23 (1967). 138-155
- 1975: Abydos, LÄ I. Wiesbaden 1975.28-41

Kitchen, K.A.
-1990: Catalogue of the Egyptian Collection in the National Museum. Rio de Janeiro. Warminster

Krauss, R.
- 1993. Zur Problematik der Nubienpolitik Kamoses sowie der Hyksosherrschaft in Oberägypten. Orientalia 62 (1993). 17-29

Lattes
- 1992: Portes pour l'au delà. L'Egypte, le Nil et le "Champ des offrandes" (Catalogue d l'exposition), Musée archaéologiques (edit. by S. Aufrère, N.Bosson, C. Landes). Lattes

Leahy, A.
- 1977: The Osiris 'Bed' Reconsidered. Orientalia 46 (1977). 424-434
- 1989: A Protective Measure at Abydos in the Thirteenth Dynasty. JEA 75 (1989). 41-60

Leprohon, R. J.
- 1985: Stelae I, The Early Dynastic Period to the Late Middle Kingdom. CAA Museum of Fine Arts Boston 2. Mainz

el-Maksoud, M. A.
- 1998: Tell Heboua (1981-1991). Paris

Marée, M.
- 1993: A remarkable Group of Egyptian Stelae from the Second Intermediate Period. OMRO 73 (1993). 7-22

Mariette, A.E.
- 1880: Catalogue général des monuments d'Abydos. Paris
- 1889: Les mastabas de l´Ancien Empire. edited by G. Maspero. Paris

Maspero, G.
- 1890: Monuments Égyptiens du Musée de Marseilles. Rec Trav 13 (1890).113-126

Martin, G. T.
- 1971: Egyptian Administrative and Private-Name Seals. Oxford
- 1979: Private Name Seals in Alnwick Castle Collection. MDAIK 35 (1979). 215-226

Mathieu, B.
- 1998: Une stèle du règne d´Amenemhat II au ouadi Um Balad (désert oriental). BIFAO 98 (1998). 235-246

de Meulenaere, H.
- 1981: Contributions à la prosopographie du Moyen Empire. BIFAO 81 (1981). Bulletin des Centenaire. 77-85
-1985: Les monuments d'un haut dignitaire de la 13e dynastie. CdE LX.119-120 (1985).75-84

Montet, P.
- 1947: Les tombeaux de Siout et de Deir Rifeh. Kemi 6 (1936). 131-163
- 1947: La nécropole royale de Tanis I. Les constructions et le tombeau d`Osorkon II à Tanis. Paris

de Morgan, J.
- 1894: Catalogue des monuments et inscriptions de l'Égypte antique.I. De la frontière de Nubie à Kom Ombos. Wien
- 1895: Fouilles à Dahchour. Mars-Juin 1894. Vienna
- 1903. Fouilles à Dahchour. 1894-1895. Vienna

Morgensen, M.
- 1918: Inscriptions hiéroglyphiques du Musée national de Copenhague / par Maria Mogensen. Copenhague
- 1919: Stèles égyptiennes au musée national de Stockholm. Copenhagen

Moss, R.
- 1933: An Unpublished Rock-tomb at Asyûṭ. JEA 19 (1933). 33

Naville, E.
- 1907: The XIth Dynasty Temple at Deir el-Bahari. Part 1. EEF 28. London
- 1910: The XIth Dynasty Temple at Deir el-Bahari. Part 2. EEF 30. London

Newberry, P. E.
- 1893: Beni Hasan I. ASE 1. London
- 1895: El Bersheh II. ASE 4. London

O'Connor, D.
- 1985: The 'Cenotaphs' of the Middle Kingdom at Abydos. in: Mélanges Gamal eddin Mokhtar. Bibliothèque d'Etude 97/2. Cairo. 161-177

Ortiz, G.
-1993: The George Ortiz collection. London

Peet, T. E.
-1914: The Cemeteries of Abydos II. 1911-1912. London

Peet, T. E. W., Loat. L.S.
- 1913: The Cemeteries of Abydos. III. London

Petrie, W. M. F.
- 1888: A Season in Egypt 1887. London
- 1889: Hawara, Biahmu and Arsinoe, London
- 1902: Abydos I. EEF 22. London
- 1903: Abydos II. EEF 24. London
- 1909: Qurneh. BSAE 16. London
- 1925: Tombs of Courtiers and Oxyrhynkhos. BSAE 37. London
- 1926: Ancient Weights and Measures. BSAE 39. London

Pierret, P.
- 1874: Études Égyptologiques deuxième Livraison. Recueil d'inscriptions inédites du Musée Égyptien du Louvre. Paris
- 1878: Recueil d'inscriptions inédites du Musée Égyptien du Louvre. Paris

Pörtner, B.
- 1908: Aegyptische Grabsteine und Denksteine aus Athen und Konstantinopel. Strassburg

Posener, G.
- 1968: Une stèle de Hatnoub. JEA 54 (1968). 67-70
- 1976: L'enseignement loyaliste. Paris

Quirke, S.
- 1990: The Administration of Egypt in the Late Middle Kingdom. New Malden
- 1991: Royal power in the 13th Dynasty. in: Middle Kingdom Studies. Edited by S. Quirke. New Malden. 123-139
- 2000: Six Hieroglyphic Inscriptions in University College Dublin. RdE 51 (2000), 223-243, pl. XXX-XXXIII

Quirke, S./Fitton, L.
- 1997: An Aegean Origin for Egyptian Spirals? Ancient Egypt, the Aegean, and the Near East: Studies in Honour of Martha Rhoads Bell, San Antonio, Texas, 421-444

Randall-MacIver. D.; Mace. A.
- 1902: El Amrah and Abydos. EEF Memoir 23. London

Reisner, G.A.
- 1923: Excavations at Kerma. IV-V. Harvard African Studies 6. Cambridge

Rosati, G.
- 1988: Le stele del Medio Regno, in Civiltà degli Egizi, le credenze religiose, edit. by Anna Maria Donadoni Roveri, Milano, 104-113

Rosati Castellucci, G.,
- 1980 L´onomastica del Medio Regno come mezzo di datazione, Aegyptus 60 (1980), 3-72

Ryholt, K.S.B.
- 1997: The Political Situation in Egypt during the Second Intermediate Period. Copenhagen

Sadek, Ashraf I.
- 1980: The Amethyst Mining Inscriptions of Wadi el-Hudi. I: Text. Warminster
- 1985: Wadi el-Hudi. II: Additional Texts, Plates. Warminster

Schmitz, B.
- 1976: Untersuchungen zum Titel sꜣ-njswt "Königssohn". Bonn

Seidel, M.
- 1994, Entry T35 in the exhibition catalogue 'Suche nach der Unsterblichkeit – Hamm'. Mainz, 94-96

Sethe, K.
- 1928: Dramatische Texte zu Altaegyptischen Mysterienspielen. Leipzig

Seyfried, K.-J.
-1981: Beiträge zu den Expeditionen des Mittleren Reiches in die Ost-Wüste. Hildesheimer Ägyptologische Beiträge 15. Hildesheim

Simpson, W. K.
- 1974: The Terrace of the Great God at Abydos: The Offering Chapels of Dynasties 12 and 13. Publications of the Pennsylvania-Yale Expedition to Egypt 5. New Heaven and Philadelphia
- 1986: Papyrus Reisner IV. Boston
- 1988: Lepsius Pyramid LV at Dahshur: the Mastaba of Si-Ese, Vizier of Amenemhet II, Pyramid studies and other essays presented to I.E.S. Edwards. Edited by John Baines, London. 57-60
- 1991: Mentuhotep, Vizier of Sesostris I, Patron of Art and Architecture. MDAIK 47 (1991). 331-340
- 1995: Inscribed Material from the Pennsylvania-Yale Excavations at Abydos. Publications of the Pennsylvania-Yale Expedition to Egypt 6. New Heaven and Philadelphia

Spalinger, A.
-1980: Remarks on the Family of Queen *Ḫᶜ.s -nbw* and the Problems of Kingship in Dynasty XIII. RdE 32 (1980). 95-116

Steckeweh, H.; Steindorff; G.
- 1936: Die Fürstengräber von Qaw. Leipzig

Stewart, H.M.
- 1979: Egyptian Stelae, Reliefs and Paintings from the Petrie Collection II. Warminster

Szafranski, Z. E.
- 1999: The Djadjawy of the Palace of Amenemhat I at Tell el-Dabᶜa. Ägypten und Levante VIII (1999). 101-106

Vernus, P.
- 1974: Une formule des shaoubtis sur un pseudo-naos de la XIIIe dynastie. RdE 26 (1974). 100-114
- 1986: Le surnom au Moyen Empire. Sudia Pohl 13. Rome
- 1994: Observations sur le titre imy-rꜣ ḫtmt >>directeur du trésor<< Grund und Boden in Altägypten. Akten des internationalen Symposiums. Tübingen 18.-20. Juni 1990. edit. by Schafik Allam. Tübingen. 251-260

Vodoz, I.
- 1978: Les scarabees graves du musée d'art et d'histoire des Geneve. Aegyptiaca Helvetica. Genève

Ward, W. A.
-1982: Index of Egyptian Administrative and Religious Titles of the Middle Kingdom. Beirut
- 1986: Essays on Feminine Titles of the Middle Kingdom and Related Subjects. Beirut

Wegner, J.
- 1995: Old & New Excavations at the Abydene Complex of Senwosret III. KMT 6(2). 1995. 59-71
- 1998: Excavations at the Town of Enduring-are-the-Places-of-Khakaure-Maa-Kheru-in Abydos: A preliminary Report on the 1994 and 1997 Seasons. JARCE XXXV (1998).1-44
- 2000: A Middle Kingdom town at south Abydos. Egyptian Archaeology 17 (2000). 8-10

Willems, H.
- 1988: Chests of Life. Den Haag

Yoyotte, J.
- 1989: Le roi Mer-djefa-Rè et le dieu Sopdou, un monument de la XIVe dynastie. BSFE 114 (1989). 17-63

Indices

1. Names

2. Titles

3. Museum objects

CG 20268, 79
CG 20282, 32, 47
CG 20286, 24, 58
CG 20309, 34, 63, 66
CG 20322, 49, 50
CG 20334, 15, 16, 25, 54, 62, 74
CG 20342, 79
CG 20350, 58
CG 20353, 45
CG 20373, 49
CG 20391, 21, 24
CG 20396, 51
CG 20418, 80
CG 20435, 15
CG 20445, 62
CG 20459, 13, 17, 71
CG 20473, 79
CG 20479, 44
CG 20486, 50
CG 20515, 2
CG 20520, 70
CG 20526, 71
CG 20530, 49
CG 20539, 7, 9, 40
CG 20540, 5
CG 20542, 2
CG 20549, 71, 79
CG 20556, 15, 42, 52, 57, 66
CG 20561, 79
CG 20562, 6, 12, 13, 15, 69
CG 20565, 57
CG 20567, 2
CG 20570, 3, 71
CG 20614, 21, 26, 33, 43-45, 52, 62, 74, 77
CG 20616, 22, 44, 51
CG 20656, 6
CG 20661, 49
CG 20666, 42, 57, 66
CG 20668, 49, 50
CG 20677, 66
CG 20693, 51
CG 20703, 61
CG 20708, 34
CG 20716, 24, 53
CG 20718, 16, 21, 23, 42, 45, 52, 58, 62, 74, 76
CG 20724, 6
CG 20732, 50
CG 20751, 2
CG 23023, 79
CG 23042, 79
CG 28030, 49
CG 28126, 49
JdÉ 39069, 72
JdÉ 43461, 65, 66, 70
pBoulaq 18, 21, 48, 52, 58

Cambridge Fitzwilliam Museum
E.SS.37, 49
E 1.1840, 23, 24, 25, 42 - 46, 51, 55, 58

Chicago Field Museum of Natural History
no. 31647, 16, 42, 62, 65, 75

Copenhagen ÆIN Ny Carlsberg Glyptotek
1539, 11

Copenhagen National Museum Ad 10, 5, 34

Dublin
UC 1360, 16, 21, 23, 42, 43, 52, 53, 54, 75
UC 1365, 57, 58, 78

Durham (ex Alnwick)
1946, 57
1941, 32, 42, 63
1984, 50, 54

Edinburgh A.1951.344, 66, 70

Florence
Florence 2500, 10, 11
Florence 2503, 67
Florence 2504, 2
Florence 2506, 3, 58
Florence 2512, 56
Florence 2523, 3
Florence 2559, 70
Florence 2561, 70
Florence 2590, 69

Hannover inv. no. 2932, 54, 67, 68, 69

Hildesheim Inv. no. 6000, 79

Leiden 6, 47
Leiden 8, 66
Leiden 13, 14, 16, 33, 42, 50, 67
Leiden 14, 14, 44, 71, 74
Leiden 15, 15, 62
Leiden 26, 77, 78
Leiden 27, 67, 69
Leiden 30, 3
Leiden 31, 67, 68, 69
Leiden 33, 33, 34
Leiden 34, 6, 22, 24, 26, 32, 33, 35, 42, 62, 63, 64, 65, 71, 74
Leiden 35, 63
Leiden 43, 70
Leiden 44, 70
Leiden 50, 3
Leiden 53, 56
Leiden 1963/8.32, 13

Liverpool no. M 13846, 57
Liverpool no. M13635, 28, 30, 48, 63, 74, 77
Liverpool no. M13661, 28. 45, 48, 76, 77

London British Museum
BM 100, 47
BM 1246, 65
BM 1348, 49
BM 162, 79
BM 202, 8
BM 210, 51, 72
BM 215, 14, 44, 62, 74, 77
BM 225, 25, 58
BM 236, 80
BM 238, 6, 23, 24, 44, 45, 47, 58, 64
BM 240, 43
BM 246, 40
BM 249, 25, 62, 71
BM 252, 15, 43, 62, 74, 77
BM 254, 34
BM 428, 27, 45, 59, 74
BM 557, 80
BM 576, 40
BM 614, 7
BM 805, 53, 54, 55
BM 831, 56
BM 903, 3, 23, 24, 44, 51, 52, 57, 58, 77
BM 1163, 49
BM 1367, 17

London Petrie Museum
UC 14430, 40
UC 14456, 6
UC 14487, 79
UC 32100, 18
UC 32104, 17, 18

Magdeburg, 34, 55, 56

Manchester 2963, 72

Marseilles no. 223, 23, 24, 44, 45, 47, 64
Marseilles no. 252, 17, 45

Meylan, 66, 71

Moscow 5350, 33, 42, 63
Moscow GM. no. 6758, 6
Moscow I Ia 5358, 49, 50

Munich 36, 23, 45, 57, 58
Munich GL WAF 34, 3, 69, 71

New York, Metropolitan Museum of Art
New York 14.2.7, 7
New York 12.182.1, 8, 40
New York 35.7.55, 49, 50
New York 68.12, 63
New York 68.14, 33, 51, 62
New York 69.30 l, 15

New York, Brooklyn Museum acc.no. 08.480.176, 34

Odessa GAM. inv. no. 52970, 5

Oldenburg 4403, 53

Oxford Q.C. 1111, 66

Paris, Bibliothèque Nationale, Cat. no. 16, 5, 6

Paris Musée Guimet no. 8, 66, 70

Paris, Louvre
Louvre 206, 69
Louvre AF 9916, 49
Louvre C 1, 47
Louvre C 2, 47
Louvre C 7, 56
Louvre C 11, 40, 41
Louvre C 12, 41
Louvre C 13, 42, 49, 50, 52
Louvre C 16-18, 67 ???
Louvre C 39, 26, 47
Louvre C 43, 34
Louvre C 45, 34, 51, 53, 57, 58
Louvre C 167, 79
Louvre C 172, 55
Louvre C 190, 49
Louvre C 249, 13, 56

Parma 177, 66

Pittsburgh Acc. 21538-38, 3
Pittsburgh Acc. 2983-6701, 6, 15, 16, 21, 22, 42, 43, 54, 74

Rio de Janeiro 627 (2419), 52, 53
Rio de Janeiro 631 (2423), 62
Rio de Janeiro 633 (2425), 6, 80
Rio de Janeiro 639 (2429), 62
Rio de Janeiro 646 (2436), 26, 33, 34, 42, 67

St. Petersburg 1063, 1064, 1075, 67
St. Petersburg 1081, 3, 58
St. Petersburg 1084, 6, 16, 21, 33, 44, 45, 74
St. Petersburg 1085, 45
St. Petersburg 1086, 66
St. Petersburg 1088, 3
St. Petersburg 5010, 44

Acknowledgement and copyright

Plate 1 and 2: Liverpool Museum M 13661 and M 13635
The Board and Trustees of the National Museum & Galleries on the Merseyside (Liverpool Museum).

Plate 3: Berlin 7311; Ägyptisches Museum u. Papyrussammlung SMB, photo by E. Grantz;

Plate 4: Vienna ÄS 140, Wien Kunsthistorisches Museum

Plate 5: Vienna ÄS 168, Wien Kunsthistorisches Museum; St. Petersburg Hermitage 5010, photo by A. Bolshakov; see also PM VIII, [801-413-600]

Plate 6: Berlin 7288; Ägyptisches Museum u. Papyrussammlung SMB, photo by E. Grantz

Plate 7 and 8: Papyrus fragments, University College London

The relation between key stelae discussed

Nḥjj	Ḫnms	Nb-jrwt	Snb-sw-mꜥ	Snbj	Rḥw-ꜥnḫ	Snnj
	jrj-ꜥt Ḫnms Wien 182	jrj-ꜥt wdpw Nb-jrwt Turin 1620				
	CG 20718	CG 20718	CG 20718			
	Cambridge E.1.1840	Cambridge E.1.1840				
jmj-r^{3} ḫtmtjw Nḥjj	jmj-r^{3} st Ḫnms	jmj-r^{3} st Nb-jrwt				rḫ-njswt Snnj
London 903	London 903	CG 20023	St. Petersburg 1084			St. Petersburg 1084
	rḫ-njswt Ḫnms			Snbj ; date: Neferhotep I		
	CG 20614			CG 20614	CG 20614	CG 20614
jmj-r^{3} pr wr Nḥjj	London 238 Marseille 223 Turin 1620			Wien ÄS 140	Wien ÄS 140	
Leiden 34				Leiden 34		
Aswan					rḫ-njswt Rḥw-ꜥnḫ, date: 6th year Sobekhotep IV	

Plate 1

Liverpool Museum M 13661

Plate 2

Liverpool Museum M 13661 and M 13635

Plate 3

Berlin 7311

Plate 4

Vienna ÄS 140

Plate 5

Vienna ÄS 168

St. Petersburg Hermitage 5010

Plate 6

Berlin 7288

Plate 7

UC 32104 (hieroglyphs by Quirke)

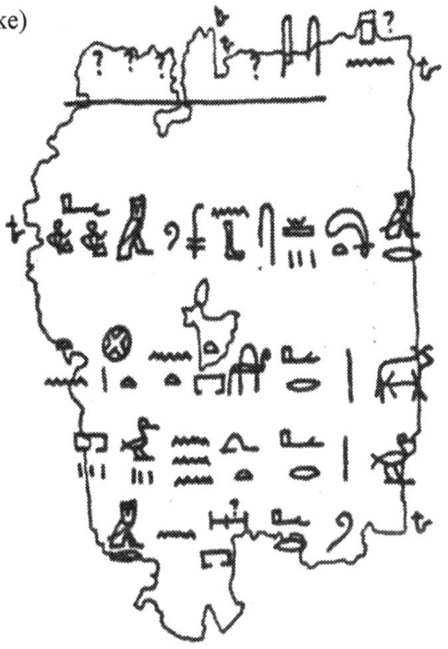

UC 32104 (hieroglyphs by Quirke)

Plate 8

UC 32100 (hieroglyphs by Quirke)

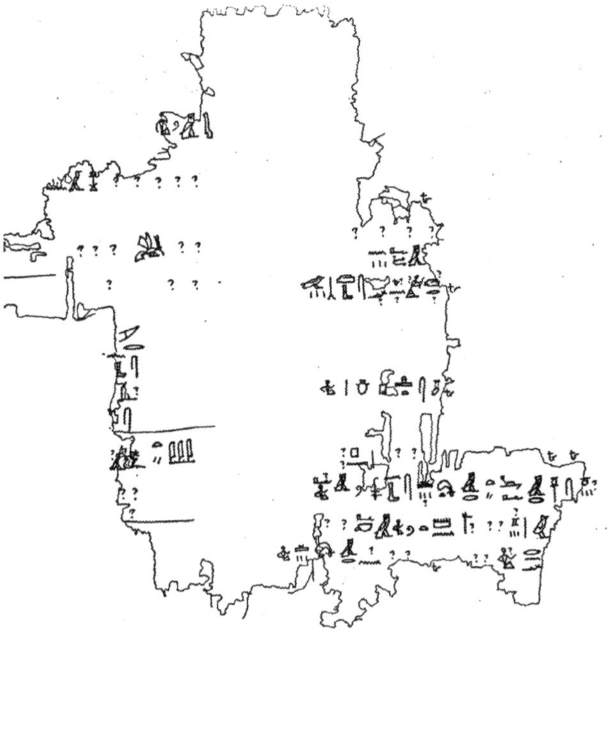

www.ingramcontent.com/pod-product-compliance
Lightning Source LLC
Chambersburg PA
CBHW061006030426
42334CB00033B/3387
* 9 7 8 1 8 4 1 7 1 2 8 6 4 *